LAUGHING GODS, WEEPING VIRGINS

Laughter in the History of Religion

LAUGHING GODS, WEEPING VIRGINS

Laughter in the History of Religion

Ingvild Sælid Gilhus

London and New York

First published 1997
by Routledge
11 New Fetter Lane, London EC4P 4EE

Simultaneously published in the USA and Canada
by Routledge
29 West 35th Street, New York, NY 10001

Typeset in Garamond by RefineCatch Limited, Bungay, Suffolk.

Printed and bound in Great Britain by Hartnolls Ltd, Bodmin, Cornwall

British Library Cataloguing in Publication Data
A catalogue record for this book is available from the British Library

Library of Congress Cataloging in Publication Data

Gilhus, Ingvild Sælid
Laughing gods, weeping virgins: Laughter in the History of
Religion / Ingvild Sælid Gilhus.
p. cm.
Includes bibliographical references and index.
1. Laughter–Religious aspects–Comparative studies.   I. Title.
BL65.L3G55 1997
291.2–dc21   96–53412

ISBN 0–415–16197–5

CONTENTS

ACKNOWLEDGEMENTS

Though the idea was conceived earlier, the actual work on this book started four years ago during a sabbatical year in Oxford. I am grateful to the University of Bergen and the Norwegian Research Council for giving me the grant that made this stay possible.

While working on the book I received valuable help from several of my colleagues. I owe special thanks to Lisbeth Mikaelsson for fruitful discussions and her comments on the manuscript during these years. I would like to thank Richard H. Pierce, Anne Stensvold, Einar Thomassen, Anne Wik and Knut Aksel Jacobsen for careful reading and helpful comments on various parts of the manuscript. I extend my thanks to the librarians at the Ashmolean Library in Oxford and the University Library in Bergen who provided me with the books I needed. I also owe my gratitude to Lauren Bryant who helped me with the editing of the manuscript and to Judith Cabot for improving its language. Part of chapter 5 includes in revised form material published in *Numen*, 37, 1, 1990. I am grateful to the editors for permission to use it here.

Finally my sincere thanks are due to my husband Nils Erik Gilhus, for his firm support, and to our children, Alette, Margrete, Kristoffer, Kaare and Ingjerd who accompanied their parents on their sabbatical.

Ingvild Sælid Gilhus
September 1996

INTRODUCTION

Religion and laughter are different kinds of human phenomena: one involves an upturned vision, the other a bodily reaction. Religion seriously addresses questions of ultimate concern; laughter is mostly unserious. In other words, religion and laughter should not go well together. But they do; there is scarcely a religion that does not include laughter in one form or another, be it in myths, rituals or theological treatises. In many religions, laughing gods, tricksters, holy fools, carnivals, comedies and clowning are stock in trade. The ludicrous makes a travesty of the sacred; when, for a short while, laughter sweeps away the holy cosmos, the divine order is exposed as an arbitrary construct.

This book is an analysis of how laughter has been used as a symbol in myths, rituals and festivals of Western religions and has thus been inscribed in religious discourse. It is *not* a book about the liberating effect of religious laughter, the joys of heaven or religious humour in general. Because my aim is to investigate a sign, not a sound, my subject is never the passing laughter of the individual, but rather, the laughter forever caught in culture and preserved; my focus is on what is written about laughter in the context of religion.

Because of its lack of decorum and its threat to orderliness, laughter has again and again been subjected to critical discourse and systematization. It has been a subject of scientific inquiry at least since the time of Plato. Greek philosophers restricted it. Christian theologians condemned it: the monks and virgins of the early Church in particular had to maintain a serious countenance. The Buddhists gave careful recommendations for how Buddhas, monks and other would-be holy men should laugh. But just as strenuously as some religions have tried to contain laughter, others have exploited its eruptive force, as seen for instance in the ancient Greek

1

cult of Dionysos, the god of laughter; in the guffawing of the Zen monks; in the Gnostics making myths about Christ's laughter at the crucifixion; in the Feast of Fools in the Middle Ages; and in today's charismatic Christian movements where people roll on the floor in the aisle of the church, overcome by unquenchable laughter. In short, laughter thrives in religions. Its ambiguity makes it an apt expression for religious experience as well as a powerful religious symbol. Like religion, laughter is situated at the intersection between body and mind, individual and society, the rational and the irrational. When laughter works itself into the religious universe, it reveals unexpected connections between elements in the religious web and creates alternative meanings to those held by the mainstream interpreters of the religion in question.

In other words, laughter is a fruitful subject for religio-historical analysis; its different modes are well worth investigation. In the history of religions, however, laughter has seldom been commented upon. Why? One answer is that scholars in the field labour under the delusion that religion is a serious business and no laughing matter. Furthermore, being often more interested in normative religion, researchers have tended not to give comical forms sufficient attention. But an equally important reason is that the history of religions has long been more concerned with studying spiritual beings than symbols and expressions rooted in human life. In this book, I want to treat laughter as a central human phenomenon that erupts in religions with irresistible power or, more instrumentally, is applied by people as a means to experience the world, categorize its forms and judge its values.

LAUGHTER, THE BODY AND TWO FIELDS OF MEANING

What is laughter? This is an impossible question to answer; laughter is many things at the same time and not the same from one culture to another. We may say that laughter is a universal human expression, restricted to humans and therefore understood as a dividing line between humankind and animals. Humans laugh when the body is tickled, and when hearing or experiencing funny things. Like crying, which can be brought about by harm to the body or by sad news, laughter is caused by stimulation of the body or by stimulation of the intellect, humorous or otherwise. There is a discrepancy, though, between the highly developed cognitive skills required to savour jokes, and the eruptive bodily reaction called laughter. Laughter is not a constant human expression with fixed meanings. On the contrary, its meanings vary. Like other human expressions, laughter is part of culture, and its place and function are culturally determined. Frequently, laughter is a result of humour, but not always. Mocking laughter has little to do with humour. And when laughter is a result of joking, as in the Greek cult of Demeter where obscene joking was ritualized, then laughter is more fully explained in relation to the cult than to humour in a limited sense. In other words, the sphere of laughter and the sphere of humour may intersect with each other, but they do not overlap completely.

Accordingly, 'humour' is not singled out here as a master key for the interpretation of laughter. In this book I have looked for important symbolic contexts in which laughter appears. One such important context, as I have noted, is the human body. In this connection we are not talking about the human body as a biological entity, but of the body as it is moulded by culture, conceived by the human mind and used as a religious symbol. The location and meaning of laughter in a particular religion are closely connected with the religion's symbolic use of the human body. Thus, one aim of this book is to show how the meaning of laughter is connected with the construction and interpretation of the body in religions through the ages.[1]

Generally speaking, the body is a large symbolic system through which thoughts and feelings about humans and their world are played out; through its surface and openings, the body connects the human and non-human worlds. Matter and symbols pour in and out through its openings. Laughter is a voluntary and extreme opening up of the human body: when one laughs uproariously, the mouth is fully opened, much more so than when speaking or eating. Because laughter is an opening of the body, it is structurally connected with other bodily openings, such as ears and eyes, and because laughter is something which pours forth from the body, it may be parallel with, for instance, sneezing, crying or ejaculation. These types of connections are exploited in religious myths and rituals, where plays on bodily openings and closures are often developed (Lévi-Strauss 1970: 125). For instance, in fertility rituals, symbols and practices connoting sexuality and birth are frequently combined with obscene joking and laughter. Symbolically, these jokes refer to how the human body must be opened up for life to flow and to make fruitful humans, animals and fields.

Laughter as an opening up also implies that it is situated on the margins of the body. It can thus fill a double function of signifying a friendly opening up to a community and a hostile closure against outsiders. Laughter explores the world's dividing lines; when laughter strikes out against what is foreign, the better to define its own, it takes the form of ridicule and blasphemy, and becomes a dangerous force. Used in strategies of oppression or resistance, laughter can be a strong religious expression and is always some sort of marker.

Because of its violent, eruptive character, laughter tends to be perceived as powerful, either destructive or life-giving. Yet it does not point to one ultimate meaning, but is rather a sign embracing many different meanings. Despite laughter's lack of fixed semantic content, however, ludicrous meanings in religion are often clustered into two opposing phenomenological fields, constituted roughly by:

1 creation and birth, joy, sexuality and eroticism; food and intoxicating drinks; feasts and comedies; dancing; ecstasy, madness and wisdom;

2 destruction and death; derision and shame; ridicule and blasphemy; tragedy.

These two fields are invested, respectively, with life-giving and destructive values. The existence of two different types of laughter begs the question of whether they have different origins. Many attempts at answering this question have taken recourse to evolutionary biology and the development of apes and primates, postulating different physiological origins for the two types of laughter, often with the explicit understanding that aggressive laughter is the more primitive type of laughter (Lorenz 1963, van Hooff 1971). The reference to apes is rather revealing; it suggests that laughter is perceived as a disturbing human phenomenon, because of its noisy display and manifold meanings, its opposition to ordinary language and its lack of fixed semantic content. These qualities, which are inherent in laughter, may create a desire to link laughter firmly with the animal sphere. But that type of move leaves us with a paradox: according to Aristotle, laughter is a characteristic of human beings, something that divides us from the animals. How can laughter both divide us from the animals and link us to the apes? In a cultural investigation such as this book, laughter's ape-connection is a dead end, as dead as the inclination to rate aggressive laughter as being more primitive than playful laughter. What is important about laughter, in

4

connection with this study, is how it appears as a rich symbolic human expression with different modes and meanings. In this book, the two fields referred to above are treated as symbolic or phenomenological fields, not to be explained away by apes' behaviour.

THEORIES OF LAUGHTER

Laughter is a versatile phenomenon and its study has been pursued in several fields, from philosophy to the social sciences and psychology. Theories of laughter deal with laughter's meanings, causes and functions, and the mechanisms involved in the production of humour. There are three main theories about why humans laugh, usually described as the superiority theory, the incongruity theory and the relief theory. Briefly:

1   the superiority theory defines laughter in the context of power over and aggression against a victim;[2]
2   the incongruity theory sees laughter as caused by two opposite meanings being held together at the same time. The obvious meaning is suddenly dropped in favour of the unexpected meaning;[3]
3   the relief theory stresses that laughter relieves psychical pressure. We laugh at forbidden things, things we usually spend energy on keeping locked up. Laughter is an expression of the relief felt when the pressure is released, thus functioning as a safety valve for the individual and society.[4]

Whatever their focus, these theories have all treated laughter as a universal phenomenon. They do not capture the subtleties of laughter's relationship to cultural meaning and change. In this study, the insights provided by these existing theories are used as tools to search for cultural and religious meanings. One example can illustrate how the theories can be helpful: when the lower priests in France in the late Middle Ages took an ass into the church, they joked and laughed (incongruity), made fools of the bishops and others who usually took them in hand (superiority) and claimed that they were as barrels of fermenting wine which would burst if they were not opened to relieve the pressure (relief) (Gilhus 1990). The 'Feast of the Ass' simultaneously bears out all of the above-mentioned theories, which in this case supplement each other beautifully. However, none of these theories explain the *meaning* of laughter in this religious feast, nor do they analyse the strategies of power and knowledge of which laughter is part. In the present analysis, I focus on the meanings of laughter, not the causes of laughter; the field of laughter more than the functions of laughter; the cultural significance of laughter rather than the psychology of emotions and cognitions in the humour process. Laughter is seen as a cultural product and an historical subject, connected to the human body as a symbol.

Even if humour has now become a special field of knowledge, a theme of annual symposia and journals,[5] we rarely find scholars who treat laughter and the body systematically as cultural constructs. But there are some: the social anthropologist Mary Douglas has correlated laughter and jokes with social forms. According to Douglas, 'disturbed bodily control mirrors both the joke structure and the social structure' (Douglas 1975: 101). Thus she makes laughter part of social analysis. In the present study, Douglas' works on laughter together with those of the Russian literary critic Mikhail Bakhtin and the German philosopher Peter Sloterdijk have been a great inspiration.

In contrast to Douglas, Bakhtin and Sloterdijk are more concerned with cultural than with social forms. As part of his analysis of Rabelais' work, Bakhtin explored the culture of laughter of the Middle Ages and the Renaissance (Bakhtin 1968). He depicted the laughter culture as a counterculture belonging to the ordinary people, and brought attention to how the meanings of the body and its processes were exploited. Peter Sloterdijk takes us back to the philosophy of the Cynics (Sloterdijk 1983). He accentuates the Cynics' uncontrolled outbursts of laughter and their identification with the body and its pleasures. Sloterdijk contrasts the original Cynics with the cynics of today: the laughter of modern cynics is a product of rational control and reflects a lack of feeling. Similar to Bakhtin's work, Sloterdijk's book is written in praise of the body, playfulness and laughter.

Bakhtin and Sloterdijk have focused on different periods in the history of laughter. Their works both contribute to the understanding of these periods, and are brilliant examples of a phenomenological and structural approach to laughter and the body. And not only past phases of laughter are illuminated in their works; their books also reflect laughter's present state in the West. When Bakhtin and Sloterdijk look back to an age when laughter was in tune with the body, their attempts to define laughter's most genuine expressions in an idealized past clearly contribute to the creation of a modern mythology of laughter. In the last part of this book, examples of what I call 'the remythologization of laughter' in modern Western thinking will be explored. Because it is intimately intertwined with contemporary religious uses of laughter, such a mythology is worth untangling.

HISTORY OF RELIGIONS

In addition to relying on previous research on laughter, this book is also indebted to the history of religions, especially its comparative branch. Comparative religion is an old approach within the broader field of history of religions. It counts researchers such as Mircea Eliade and James Frazer among its fathers. In the course of the last century, comparative religion has been going in and out of style while struggling to strike a balance between the universal and the cultural, the systematic and the historical. It has been very difficult to find a balance between universal patterns and cultural meanings, and very easy to break one's scholarly neck in trying to do so. Still, I will attempt in this book a comparative, rather than an historical investigation, but in a more modest manner than earlier comparativists have done.

In the following chapters, I describe main tendencies and perspectives from the Western history of laughter. To describe those tendencies, I do not attempt a systematic historical survey. Rather, I concentrate on three different cultural periods: the Ancient Near East and Classical Greek cultures, the Hellenistic culture and Western Christianity, and the modern period. These periods and the religions they have generated are distinguished from each other by different world-views and different conceptions of human beings and the human body. Subsequently, they reveal three interpretative contexts for laughter's religious roles. The symbolic and religious uses of laughter are not static within these different periods; they developed over these long periods of time and are part of general historical processes. But my focus is not on small-scale historical events, it is rather on what is representative from each period.

The three periods are regarded as distinct from each other, but it would be wrong to separate the periods by absolute dates; a flexible view on how they blend into each other is in order. Still, we witness an obvious turn in the conception of laughter in the fourth century BC in Greece, parallel with the transformation of the Greek Classical culture into Hellenistic culture, where for the first time laughter became an object of philosophical criticism and attempts at control. Something similar happened at the beginning of the modern period, as seen in Descartes and Hobbes, when laughter again became an object for philosophical thought and was treated very critically (Morreall 1989). In the twentieth century, laughter's cultural value has again changed, and it is now treated as positive and desirable.

The fourth century BC and the sixteenth–seventeenth century AD also mark periods of great cultural and religious transformation. This transformation is in turn reflected in how conceptions of laughter changed at roughly the same time. Within the above-mentioned major periods – Ancient Near East and Classical Greece; Hellenism and Western Christianity; and the modern period – certain dominant contexts contribute greatly to determining laughter's ritual use and religious meanings. These dominant interpretative contexts are, respectively, the cosmos in Ancient Near East and Greek religion, where laughter partakes in the creation and maintenance of the world; the body in Hellenism and Western Christianity where laughter is mainly conceived in the context of body and spirit and in the drama of individual salvation; and the mind or psyche in the modern period where laughter comes to be connected with the rationality of human beings and with health, happiness and knowledge.

In each period, laughter has distinct cultural and religious roles to play, which may be considered in the form of types and subtypes. While one type characterizes a period and what is dominant in that period, this does not mean that the type is non-existent in other periods; there are universal traits in laughter and links between the periods. One example will illustrate what I mean. Rituals of regeneration and fertility are typical for the pre-Christian period, and a regenerative laughter is frequently found in such rituals. But we also meet the so-called *risus paschalis* in late Medieval Europe; the laughter of Easter day is called forth by the officiating priest who makes jokes for the congregation. This laughter was connected to the resurrection of Christ, and was obviously intended to release life-giving forces in humans and nature. In this way, it had much in common with the regenerating laughter of the earlier period.

But before we proceed to a more detailed study of the different types of laughter in each period, an overview of the periods may be helpful.

THREE CULTURAL CONTEXTS OF RELIGIOUS LAUGHTER

The Ancient Near East and Classical Greek cultures

Middle Eastern and Mediterranean high cultures were characterized by cosmological thinking. Myths and rituals focused on the creation and maintenance of the world, and on the place of humans within the world. What Jean-Pierre Vernant has said about the Greeks, that they were 'spontaneously cosmic' and that their being was 'a being-in-the-world', could easily apply to their neighbours as well (Vernant 1995: 16, 12, Finnestad 1987).

The links that existed between humans and the animate universe surrounding them were expressed in several ways. One important way to express this cosmological connection was through the body. The physical body was necessary for life: without their bodies, the dead had to endure a miserable existence as shadows beneath the earth in the realms of the Mesopotamian Ereshkigal or the Greek Hades. But the body was not only necessary to maintain human life, it was also important in maintaining the world. The consubstantiality believed to exist between the body and the universe, implying that the body and the world were interconnected, reflecting and influencing each other, had wide-ranging implications. From the dead bodies of slain gods or from their blood, the world and human beings were created; the copulation of gods brought new gods into being. Mummified human bodies also had cosmic significance. One of the common traits among the cultures of the Mediterranean area and the Ancient Near East is the exploitation of human and animal bodies as a means to describe, explore and maintain the connections between humans and the world. The sacrifice of the animal connected the human and the divine (Burkert 1972, Girard 1977). The entrails of animals were mirrors of the future – the animal liver was a source of oracular wisdom for the Mesopotamians, while the Romans read the future by observing the flight of birds.

If the body was consubstantial with the world, then human beings changed the world when they acted upon it. Joyful laughter made the world vibrate with life. Laughter was a cosmic force. Linked to eroticism, laughter created and recreated the world, as seen in rituals of the Greek Demeter. Ridicule and mocking laughter kept the individual contained within a hierarchy of human and divine powers, as seen in the Mesopotamian deities' treatment of the

9

human hero Adapa. These two types of laughter will be discussed later as the laughter of regeneration and the laughter of derision, and we will pursue different subvariants of these types in chapters on the cultures of the Mediterranean and the Near East.

In regenerative and derisive laughter, laughter's power is used in a controlled way. But laughter is always eruptive, and sometimes this eruption escapes attempts to control it. Laughter can become a dangerous destabilizing power, and may change the fate of human beings and their world. That power is seen in the Greek god Dionysos. In his cult, laughter reached out to that which was not yet thought and had never been described. Thus it touched the chaotic dimensions of being in which human existence was grounded, a chaos which humans so desperately struggled to keep at bay.

The Hellenistic culture and Western Christianity

The significance of cosmological laughter was challenged by the different religions of the Roman Empire. From the ashes of religious relativity rose Christianity, and laughter became embroiled in the Christian split between body and soul. As the body became ambiguous, laughter became dubious and the object of fierce debate.

The changes in the traditional concept of the body had their prehistory in antiquity when the concept of humanity underwent a process of profound transformation.[6] In ancient times, the body was generally regarded as of lower value; the Orphics saw it as the tomb. The threefold hierarchy of heaven, earth and the underworld had been changed by the Ptolemaic cosmic image in which the earth was surrounded by the planetary spheres. The human body was made of matter and had much in common with the animal world, but the soul was related to the planets and the stars. According to widely held opinions on death, the soul would go to its ultimate destiny among the stars and reach a celestial immortality, or be transposed to an intelligible world. While the body returned to earth, less developed souls would return to new bodies – animal or human. During life, the rational soul should ideally rule the body. However, the material organism was not without importance. On the contrary, it had to be kept fit and healthy to be in harmony with humans' rational principle and with the universe in general (Corrigan 1986).

The Christians, starting with Paul, began to deprive the cosmos of its sacredness. In the Christian vision, the stars of heaven lost their power and humans stood alone, singled out among all species as the only one made in the image of God. But in Christianity, the body also acquired a new meaning; it was simultaneously conceived of as a burden, a challenge and a vehicle of salvation. In opposition to nearly all philosophies of body and soul at the time, Christianity maintained that the body was destined for salvation. For that destiny, the body had to be continually worked upon, changed and reshaped.

The crucified saviour and his bodily resurrection was the core of the creed of the early Christian Church, and the focus of its rituals. From the first proclamation of the resurrected Christ, a continuous discourse on the body followed. It included theological debates on the nature of Christ; the exemplary ascetic life of virgins, monks and Desert Fathers; the preoccupation with the blood of the martyrs and the cult of the relics; the debates on the meaning of the Lord's Supper; the introduction of the Feast of Corpus Christi; the staging of the mystery plays; and on and on all the way to the Reformation. The human body had indeed become a rich religious symbol; bodily resurrection stood forth as 'a concept of sublime courage and optimism' (Bynum 1995: 343). The importance of the body's symbolic value would last for centuries, and laughter was rapidly drawn into this context.

The old cosmological laughter had been both vertical and horizontal. It had kept the ups up, and the downs down, that which was inside inside, and that which should stay out out. It had made life flow when it ran dry; in Greece it most significantly touched the dimensions of that which was unthought. Cosmological laughter had been situated in the world, defining the world and keeping it moving; not so with Christianity. Christian laughter was inserted at the meeting point between body and soul and drawn into theological discourse both as an object of judgement and as a subject used to pass judgement. Laughter was related differently to the body, dependent on whether those who laughed took their stand with the spirit (as in Gnosticism), with the body (as in the carnivals of the Middle Ages) or with both (as in the English mystery plays). Because laughter in Western Christianity became more explicitly part of the discourse on the body, its functions and meanings can be more systematically related to main conceptions of the body in this religion. As Christian concepts of the body developed during the Middle Ages, so also did concepts of laughter. From being a marginal phenomenon in the early Church, laughter moved into the centre of Medieval culture. In Western Christianity, we find Gnostic laughter, which is spiritual and belongs to the first part of our period, and the embodied laughter of carnival, which belongs to the late Middle Ages.

The modern period

Complex historical and cultural processes worked together to limit laughter. Conceptions of the body changed over time. From the end of the Middle Ages, the body's natural processes had been gradually hidden and made private (Elias 1978). Because to an increasing degree uncontrolled laughter was associated with the body, laughter was looked upon with dislike and attempts were made to suppress it. One sphere in which these attempts met with considerable success was in religion. The Protestants were pious and served their God by means of the word. Their services tended to be solemn and serious, and joking was often explicitly forbidden. The Protestant attitude had much in common with that which dominated in the early Church and the first part of the Middle Ages. But this attitude came to be challenged. In the twentieth century, laughter has been associated with humour, and especially with the human ability to perceive incongruity: 'I think, therefore I laugh' (Paulos 1985). As it has moved from the sphere of the body to that of reason and the mind, the status of laughter has changed dramatically.

Today it is a matter of course that laughter is good for human beings. This is a message our culture transmits through several channels: medical, sociological, philosophical and psychological. While in earlier centuries laughter was criticized, being connected to stupidity or the division between conquerors and victims, today's laughter promotes liberation and play. From a medical point of view, laughter is regarded as relaxing muscles and relieving the brain; it fosters health and happiness. The social sciences join in: functional theories clarify how well laughter serves social ends. By means of such concepts as 'joking relationships', 'clowns' and 'tricksters', and 'rituals of rebellion', these sciences show how hostility is vented in a harmless way by means of ritualized laughter. The moral in these anthropological stories is that within its defined space, laughter is good for society.

Because laughter has been re-evaluated and is now generally regarded as healthy, equally good for individual and society, it has been reintroduced into religion as a legitimate religious expression.

In the Christianity of the present day, laughter is reflected in sketches, comics, joke-books, books about holy fools in general, and about Jesus as clown in particular.

Parallel with this development in the Christian tradition of safe and healthy laughter, laughter is also present in the orientalizing trend in the West. Here laughter includes a laughter of wisdom, especially inspired by Buddhism. It is seen, for instance, in Zen Buddhism, with its jokes and belly laughter and in the smiling countenance of the Dalai Lama. A more explicit variant of 'the-laughter-of-oriental-wisdom' theme is the jocular laughter of the recent guru Bhagwan Sri Rajneesh and his followers. Therapeutic laughter is typical for our time and will, like its predecessors in the history of religious laughter, be described and evaluated in the following chapters.

To summarize briefly, the leading questions of this investigation are: what types of laughter exist in religions? What are their meanings? In what ways is the meaning of laughter in religions connected with how the body has been moulded by culture and used as a religious symbol through the ages? In the wake of these main problems, there arise numerous additional questions to be explored, including: is laughter in religions mainly used as a bridge between the human and the divine or is it rather a human rebellion against God? Is it a mechanism of cultural control or a vehicle for the unexpressed? Why was laughter accepted as a religious expression in some periods and condemned in others? It is to these and other questions that we now turn.

1

THE ANCIENT NEAR EAST
Laughter of derision and laughter of regeneration

Nobody knows when humans began to laugh, nor does anybody know when a concept of 'laughter' originated. It is possible to discern early religions in prehistoric tombs, burials and remains of buildings, but the sound of laughter has died away. Laughter is not preserved in artifacts, so we are forced to focus on symbols of laughter and narratives of laughter, acknowledging that they are different from the laughter of the living. The most ancient laughter in our world is found in myths. As narratives about the connection between gods, humans and the world, the best myths are universal and entertain people across cultures and through the centuries, at the same time as they are intimately intertwined with the culture in which they originated and the people that used them. Their transmittal to us is dependent on writing. How textual laughter stands in relation to actual laughter in ancient cultures is unknown. It is, however, reasonable to regard the ancient texts as indicative of what these societies regarded as significant contexts of laughter (Foster 1974, Römer 1978, Kraus 1960).

LAUGHTER AND TRICKERY

The earliest recorded laughter exists in the context of divine male power. The laughter of the Mesopotamian head of the gods, Anu, cunningly keeps humans in their place and the laughter of the Hittite deity Kumarbi strives for supremacy in the divine world. Anu's laughter is found in the myth about Adapa, written in Akkadian on a tablet of clay from the fifteenth or fourteenth century BC.[1]

The wise Adapa, a priest in Eridu, was out fishing to provide offerings for the altar of Ea, the god of the life-giving fresh waters. Ea was known for his wisdom and magical knowledge. He had

14

introduced humans to the benefits of civilization and was by and large the friend of humankind. Like the other Mesopotamian gods, he received daily attendance in the temple and had food served at his altar (Kramer and Maier 1989). Ea had given wisdom to Adapa, but not eternal life. As Adapa was out on the sea, the South Wind went for his boat and overturned it. Adapa cursed the South Wind. The curse was immediately effective; the wing of the South Wind broke, and for seven days no wind blew over the sea. When Anu, the enigmatic god of heaven, learned that Adapa had stopped the Wind, he became furious and summoned Adapa before his throne. Before Adapa went, Ea advised him to let his hair be unkempt and to clothe himself in mourning. Ea informed Adapa that when he arrived at the gates of heaven he would be asked by its two keepers, Dumuzi and Gizzida, why he was in mourning. To this Adapa should answer that it was because Dumuzi and Gizzida had disappeared from the land. The two flattered gods would look at each other and laugh a lot, and they would put in a plea for Adapa before Anu. Standing before the throne of Anu, Adapa would be offered the Bread of Death and the Water of Death. Ea advised Adapa not to eat or drink, but to accept a garment and anoint himself with the oil they would also offer him.

Adapa did as he was advised, and everything happened as Ea had said, except for one thing: the food which Adapa was offered was not what Ea had said it would be. On the contrary, he was offered the Bread and the Water of *Life*. However, he acted according to the advice that Ea had given and refused to eat, whereupon the god of heaven laughed at Adapa and mocked him:

> Anu watched him and laughed at him,
> 'Come, Adapa, why didn't you eat? Why didn't you drink?
> Didn't you wish to be immortal?'
>
> (Dalley 1989: 187)

In his defence, Adapa said that Ea had bidden him not to eat or drink, and Anu ordered Adapa to be sent back to earth. Ironically, the rest of the tablet is broken, and the end is missing.

People in Mesopotamia had no belief in a blessed hereafter; on the contrary, they believed that the gods did not wish them to be immortal, any more than Jahweh in the Old Testament wanted Adam and Eve to eat from the Tree of Life and live forever. Human beings were created to serve the gods, as Adapa served Ea by providing the god with food. When they were dead, they led a miserable shadowy existence beneath the earth, sitting in darkness and eating dust. The Mesopotamian myths thus comment upon the themes of life, death and immortality. In the myth of Adapa, death loomed large after the wing of the South Wind broke. Death is represented in the shape of Dumuzi and Gizzida, gods who usually stayed in the underworld; it is present in the clothes of mourning and the unkempt hair of Adapa; and in Ea's references to the Water and Bread of Death. Life is symbolized by the gown and the oil Anu gave Adapa. Immortality is present by being absent: Ea had not made Adapa immortal, and Adapa was cheated out of the Water and Bread of Life.

Trickery is obviously at the core of the narrative; there are at least two frauds in the myth, and both are due to Ea. The first fraud occurs when Adapa tells Dumuzi and Gizzida that it was for their sake that he was dressed in mourning. We know that the clothes of mourning were no true expression of grief, but a trick to make Dumuzi and Gizzida intercede for Adapa with Anu. Their laughter is an answer to Adapa's attempts to flatter them. The second and vital fraud is the food Adapa was offered; either it carried death as Ea said, or it was life-giving, as Anu said. In both cases, Adapa was tricked.

Most probably, Adapa was cheated out of immortality because his master, the cunning Ea, tricked him. Apparently Ea did not want Adapa to become immortal, either because he had not the power to make him so himself or because he would then lose Adapa's service. In that case Anu's laughter was a twofold mockery: it mocked Adapa who had wrongly distrusted Anu and confused immortality with mortality; and it mocked the petty Ea who did not wish his favourite to become immortal:[2] Why Anu bothered to offer Adapa immortality in the first place is an open question. Perhaps he wished to make fools out of Adapa and Ea, or wanted to keep Adapa in heaven because he had become too clever to stay on earth. If this was the case, Anu's laughter was in anger (Bing 1984). In any case, the laughter gave vent to the tension which had built up after the wing of the South Wind was broken, causing death, life and immortality to be played out against each other. Adapa was made the pawn in a divine game where divine power showed its superiority at the expense of a human victim.

The divine laughter was hardly a nice laughter.[3] The verb 'laugh' (*sahu*) in Akkadian texts is on the whole used mostly in connection with others' misfortunes. When Anu laughed and thus showed his superiority, this agrees with other occurrences of laughter in Akkadian texts. For example, when the god Nergal courts the goddess of the underworld, Ereskhigal, his lust and flirtation have a strong touch of this superiority when he laughs, seizes her by her hair and draws her to bed (Dalley 1989: 176).

In the myth of Adapa, Anu's laughter is contrasted with Adapa's curse at the South Wind. Through his curse, Adapa upset the order of the world; Anu's ridicule and laughter bring the scales again into balance. The laughter of the myth supports the hierarchy of power: when Adapa flatters the two gods of the underworld to make them laugh, he seeks the co-operation of gods who are more powerful than he. The most powerful in the world of gods and humans is Anu. His laughter precipitates Adapa's return from the realm of the divine to his normal place in the world. Anu's laughter is derisive, but not destructive: the result is that Adapa returns to life. That the Assyrian version of the myth is adapted to a magical ritual, with the purpose of curing illness in a shoulder, indicates that the end of the myth was regarded as a happy one (Burkert 1992). As the wing of the South Wind apparently healed, the shoulder would also heal. In both cases, things went back to normal.

The laughter of the two flattered subordinate gods and the laughter of Anu are all part of a game of power whose effect is to uphold the hierarchy and ensure stability. Mesopotamian societies were hierarchic, as was the world of the gods, with Anu watching over the dignity of the kingdom and the king acting as the head of the state. The difference between gods and men was enormous, as was the difference between king and servant. Divine order ruled the world, and the fate of each person was determined in advance. Even if this fate could be discovered through divination, and modified through prayer to the guardian spirits, the basic laws of existence, for instance that man was mortal and gods immortal, could not be changed. The mocking laughter of Anu was conservative. That it was also laughter at the expense of humans comes as no surprise, nor does the fact that Adapa returned to earth and mortality.

Not all divine laughter in the Ancient Near East reflected superior gods stable in their hierarchical positions. In a Hittite translation of a Hurrian myth, we encounter the laughter of Kumarbi, the son of Anu, and it occurs in a myth about the succession of gods.[4] In the myth, Kumarbi attacks his father, Anu, the king of heaven. Anu flies towards the sky, but Kumarbi rushes after him, drags him down, bites off his genitals and swallows them: 'When Kumarbi had swallowed the "manhood" of Anu, he rejoiced and laughed out loud' (Hoffner 1990: 40).

The acts of utter degradation, dethroning and castration, are accompanied by Kumarbi's triumphant laughter. His triumph turns sour, however, when Anu tells Kumarbi that by swallowing his genitals, he has been made pregnant from Anu's seed and will bear new gods (Leick 1991: 106–7). Kumarbi immediately spits out some of Anu's 'manhood', and thereby gods are born from earth. But he still has to give birth to the Weather-god, through the 'good place', probably his phallus (Kirk 1970: 213–20). Eventually Anu and the Weather-god overthrow Kumarbi.

In this myth, Kumarbi obviously overreached himself and suffered defeat. His laughter, like that of Anu in the Adapa myth, reflects the importance of hierarchy and power in the division of gods and men in the Mesopotamian and Hurrian worlds. But in contrast to Anu's laughter in the Mesopotamian myth, Kumarbi's laughter in the end reveals itself to have been a mistake. In both the Adapa and the Kumarbi myth, laughter is connected with power. By combining laughter with the biting off of genitals, the Kumarbi myth gives divine laughter a truly aggressive edge. Curiously, through the pregnancy of Kumarbi, this myth also reveals other aspects of ancient laughter, of regeneration, fertility and growth.

CREATION, CHANGE AND CONTROL

In Egyptian texts, laughter (*zbt*) is rare, and seldom connected with humour (Gugliemi 1979, 1980, van de Walle 1969). When it does occur, Egyptian laughter is often derisive and is an expression of superiority, though it may also be regenerative and creative.

In one Egyptian myth laughter is clearly erotic and represents a turning point in the narrative.[5]

The gods Horus and Seth had fought over who should inherit the throne of Egypt. The high council of the gods, the holy Ennead, tried to negotiate a peace, but the gods of the council came to blows and the audacious god Baba even mocked the sun god Re, saying, 'Your shrine is empty!' When no one served in the temples of the gods, it meant that the gods were no longer taken seriously. Baba could not have said anything more injurious; Re promptly lay down on his back, and his heart was sore (Sørensen 1991: 3–9). The Ennead was angry with Baba and rebuked him, 'Go away: you have committed a very great crime', and everyone went to their tents. Re remained on his back, sulking in solitude. Then Hathor, the goddess of sexuality and birth, went up to Re. She stood before him and uncovered her nakedness: Re burst out in laughter, rose and returned to the council.

In this myth, the exposure of the female body makes the god laugh. Like the hierarchic laughter of superiority and derision, such erotic laughter is a repeated motif. It is often triggered by an unexpected display of the naked female body, accompanying and often causing a dramatic turning point in a divine or/and human drama. Erotic laughter fights on the side of life against death, and initiates a new beginning.[6]

The combination of sexuality and laughter was not restricted to myths; it was also found in rituals. Herodotus mentions that when women worshipped Artemis in Egypt, mockery and indecent exposure were part of the ceremonies (*Historiae*, II, 59–60). In many parts of the world, professional jokers have participated in funerals to cheer up the mourners and counteract the rule of death, and their activity often involved obscene behaviour. Indecent joking and embarrassing words and gestures were believed to stimulate the forces of life, promote fertility and avert evil spirits. In the Egyptian myth of Re and Hathor, when the goddess removed her clothes, showed her body and paraded her sexuality, her behaviour violated cultural norms and kindled a sexual response expressed as laughter. Laughter symbolized the god's opening up to life and regeneration.

The regenerative aspect of laughter makes it a useful symbol in myths of creation as well. Through centuries and millennia, the Egyptians developed and refined their different myths about the creation of the world (Sauneron and Voyotte 1959: 2–91, Lesko 1991: 87–122). Creation could, for instance, take place through pre-existent matter, through the creative word or by the creator bringing forth primeval matter from his own body. In the old Heliopolitan cosmogony, alluded to in texts from different periods, the god Atum impregnated himself and ejaculated Shu and Tefnut from his mouth. They were the first gods, and from them and their children other gods were born. But if gods could be sneezed out or spat out, they could just as well be laughed out. According to a late version of this myth, the gods were born from laughter, while humans came into beings from the tears of the god of creation.[7] The parallel between spitting and sneezing, and tears, suggests that laughter is conceived of as a sort of primeval matter. Since laughter is a dynamic power, it can also be linked with the creative word.

Creation by means of words can be viewed as a creation by the mind at the expense of the body. If the words are precise, they show the creator god's sovereign control. Jahweh created in this way when he did his six days' work and said, '"Let there be light"; and there was light'. The rationality of the god is emphasized at the cost of divine emotions or body. But words do not need to be rational, they can also be mere sounds, powerful nonsense with magical effects, a point on a sliding scale between laughter and speech. Both nonsense and laughter are sounds, both lack precise meanings, but both may have an eruptive force which can create the world. In Egypt, creative laughter was paralleled by creation through words. The motif of the creative laughter and the motif of the creative word have a similar function. According to a late myth, the Egyptian goddess Mehet-weret created the world by means of seven words which went out of her mouth (Sauneron and Voyotte 1959: 31, Kákosy 1982: 3–4); while in one of the magical texts from Roman times, 'A sacred book called "Unique", or "Eighth Book of Moses"', seven gods were created from seven bursts of laughter ejaculated by a superior god (Betz 1986: 172–89, Smith 1984). This superior god is nameless. It is never said what the cause of his laughter was. Anyhow, from his 'CHA CHA CHA CHA CHA CHA CHA', seven gods were born. They were the gods of light, water, mind, generative power, fate, time and soul.

When a god laughs seven times and the seven bursts of laughter create seven new gods, the creative power of laughter is not only exploited but also kept in check. This is in conformity with the ancient wisdom teaching in Egypt that warned against exaggerated laughter and *Schadenfreude*; but if one's superiors laughed, it was important to laugh with them. It was not laughter in itself that the teachers of wisdom wanted to quench – in a time of upheaval and social unrest, the sages complained that man had lost the ability to laugh – but they wanted laughter to be kept under control. The Egyptians preferred to live in an orderly world where everything had its right place and its right time; nothing should be too much and nothing too little. They had controlled the flooding of the Nile and used it for their purpose for centuries. Thus they knew a great deal about the relationship between untamed power on the one hand and systematic order on the other. Uncontrolled bursts of divine laughter might bring forth a disorderly world.

Interestingly, the myth of laughter creating seven gods comes in the middle of a magical ritual. The magician had great ambitions; his purpose was to conjure up the highest god of the universe to be his helper. The ritual was elaborate with long preparations and many ingredients. The magician had to purify himself for forty-one days. The spell had to be said in Aries, when the moon was dark, in a house on ground level where no one had died during the past year, and with a door facing west, where the god would enter. On the floor, the magician was to build an earthen altar. He had to have wood of cypress, ten pine cones full of seed, two white roosters and two lamps, each holding an eighth of a pint of good oil. There were to be seven types of incense, seven types of flowers, figures made of flour, magical sounds, and drawings. The conjurings were many and the names of gods were invoked as the ritual proceeded.

This lengthy procedure illustrates that Egyptian magic had a recipe that had to be followed in every detail, otherwise the magic would not work or the result would be unpredictable. Thus it would not have been appropriate to have a god whose laughter was uncontrolled. What was needed was a god who laughed exactly seven times and then was quiet. The magician got it both ways; he made the most out of the creative potential of laughter without losing control.

GODS AND HUMAN BEINGS

What type of relationship between gods and human beings does the laughter in these Ancient Near Eastern myths indicate?

First of all, the gods went to great lengths to demonstrate that they transcended human laws and norms. When Adapa was fooled, and Anu laughed at him, it was the god's right because humans were weak and mortal while gods were omnipotent and eternal. Anu's laughter was a confirmation of what was generally known. The ancient peoples did not doubt their gods' power to laugh, it was an expression of their divine power. The gods had laughter in common with human beings, but divine laughter revealed the gods' superiority over humans. Laughter did not bridge the human and the divine world, but rather, made a division between them.

In the mythological texts we have examined thus far, laughter is a force keeping the human under divine control. But it is also a bubbling source of sexuality and creativity, making and remaking the world. These myths featuring divine laughter try out different ways of understanding existence. Creation is incomprehensible, but laughter is no poorer explanation than the creative word or clay. In other words, the laughter of Ancient Near Eastern myths is a purposeful type of laughter that is either derisive and controlling or regenerative.

Derisive laughter had a victim. It was frequently triggered by an incongruity between the victim's personal ambition and his cosmic or social position, or by the victim being fooled. It sometimes involved goddesses, but was mainly a male laughter of power and domination over others and included a prominent aspect of trickery. It is found in connection with an obsequious laughter – that of flattery and subordination – used to keep one's superiors amused. In the Egyptian and Mesopotamian texts, derisive laughter is most evident, corresponding to the strong hierarchical nature of these societies where humans should know their place and keep it.

Regenerative laughter had various forms. Erotic laughter was complex and ambiguous. Triggered by the nude female body and by indecencies and obscenities of women, erotic laughter thrived on an interplay of sexual forces. Creative laughter exploited the eruptive power of laughter. Magical laughter was, when it came to dynamic power, an extension of creative laughter. Creative and magical laughter were instrumental, springing from mind rather than body, and therefore were controlled rather than eruptive.

What happens when the symbolic value of erotic laughter is confronted by laughter of hierarchy and power? Examples of such a confrontation are found in the Old Testament.

JAHWEH AND THE BATTLE AGAINST EROTIC LAUGHTER

Laughter in the Old Testament stands out in comparison to laughter in other Ancient Near Eastern myths, not because Jahweh lacks a sense of humour – that was not a remarkable trait of other Ancient Near Eastern gods either – but because the divine laughter of the Old Testament is more derisive than that of any other god. [8]

A classification of biblical humour in general shows that, like 'laughter' in Mesopotamia and Egypt, most instances veer towards scorn and ridicule, not merriment and joy.[9] Divine laughter in the Old Testament is a mocking laughter. The biting irony of the prophets belongs to the same context; the aim was to mock the destruction of Jahweh's enemies. Their god did not indulge in comedy and joyful laughter, and erotic ritual laughter was regarded as an abomination. While laughter in sexual contexts had sounded abundantly in the cult of the great Baal, Jahweh's divine predecessor in Canaan (Hvidberg 1962), the prophets of Jahweh were fiercely against agrarian cults containing sexual rites. Their god worked in history, not in nature (Loretz 1990).

Many interpreters have explained Canaanite religion in terms of fertility and especially in terms of a ritual seasonal cycle connected with the death and resurrection of Baal. According to their inter-pretation, the death of Baal in Canaan, when all life withered away on earth, was accompanied by intense weeping. The cultic sorrow was followed by ecstatic joy and laughter when the god ascended from the mountain of death, the rain started to fall and the earth was again made green.

Even though this interpretation of Baal as exclusively a seasonal god has been criticized and the Baal cycle is no longer regarded as organized according to a single annual cycle, Baal was still, as king of the gods, the one who mediated the blessings of the natural cosmos to humans as well as to gods. His kingship brought life to the world. In his cult, cosmological, seasonal and political aspects converged (Smith 1994: 58–114). In the Canaanite texts the words for joy and laughter are frequently repeated and bear witness to a mythological context for Baal in which sorrow and death were contrasted with life and laughter (Hvidberg 1962: 55, Loretz 1990: 166). Later, the prophets of Israel accused the Canaanite cults of sexual licence and drunkenness because the Israelites took part in fertility rituals marked by laughter and sexual practices. The prophets were full of condemnation:

> Do not rejoice, O Israel!
> Do not exult/as other nations do;
> for you have played the whore, departing
> from your God.
> You have loved a prostitute's pay
> on all threshing floors.

> (Hosea 9:1)

The relation between the cults of Baal and the cult of Jahweh is, according to the Bible, one of opposition.[10] Unfortunately, neither ancient Ugaritic texts nor the Bible give any clear picture of how the cult of Jahweh sprang up. Was Jahweh once an Israelitic Baal? What is evident is that the prophets of Jahweh severely criticized the

Canaanite fertility cults, rejecting the old assembly of the gods as well as the queen of heaven.[11] No other god than Jahweh was to be worshipped. In relation to Western Semitic religion generally, the cult of Jahweh was a protest cult.

In Syrian–Israelite Canaan, both women and the goddess had played important roles (Loretz 1990: 121, Keel and Uehlinger 1993). In the new monotheism, women were shut out of the cult, and fertility rites containing weeping and laughter were banished.[12] In the cult created by the prophets of Jahweh, their god was differentiated from his divine contemporaries in Palestine and Syria in one important way: by rejecting sexual rituals and cultic erotic laughter. Jahweh's divine laughter was the derisive laughter of male power.

A confrontation between erotic laughter and the divine laughter of derision is illustrated in the first occurrence of laughter in the Old Testament, the narrative of the birth of Isaac. The episode concerns fertility and the sexuality of a woman, but the context is far from erotic: when Sarah was made pregnant, sexuality and fertility were made objects of the manipulative power of Jahweh. The laughter of the husband was heard first: God promised the patriarch Abraham that he and his wife, Sarah, would have a son. Abraham was then in his hundredth year and Sarah in her ninetieth: 'Then Abraham fell upon his face, and laughed' (Genesis 17: 17). Later Sarah overheard the news from the tent door and laughed to herself, '"After I have grown old, and my husband is old, shall I have pleasure?"' (Genesis 18: 10–12).

God heard Sarah and asked Abraham if anything was too hard for the Lord. Sarah had obviously laughed at the wrong time. Because she feared the consequences, she denied that she had laughed. 'No; but you did laugh', insisted God (Genesis 18:16). Though Abraham had fallen on the ground because of his laughter, God did not take him to task. In order to make a reasonable account for the incongruity between God's reaction to Sarah's laughter and his reaction to Abraham's, later commentators have said that Abraham did not laugh out of disbelief, but because he was so astonished and happy (Resnick 1987: 91). One year later Sarah bore Isaac. With that birth God's omnipotence triumphed over the disbelieving laughter of a woman. The name Isaac illustrates the point, being connected with the Hebrew word for laughter. Sarah exclaimed, 'God has made laughter for me; every one who hears will laugh over me' (Genesis 21: 6). Sarah's words reflect the two different meanings of laughter, the happy and joyful and the more derisive. Commentators have differed in their translation of Genesis 21: 6b. Will those who hear about the birth laugh with Sarah or at her? The Hebrew expression is ambiguous and has been interpreted in both ways (von Rad 1972: 230–1). Is the old woman joyfully surprised or ashamed to have become a mother? The ambiguity of the text reflects that laughter is an open symbol, not easily restricted to one meaning.

Several forms of laughter intertwine in this narrative: Abraham and Sarah's disbelieving laughter before their child was born, Sarah's laughing joy when Isaac came and her foreboding of the mocking laughter of others when they heard about her giving birth. The aspects of these forms of laughter – disbelief, joy and mockery – are swept away by the triumphant laughter of God, which is echoed in the name Isaac. Though this divine laughter accompanies the birth of a child, it has little to do with the cultic laughter of fertility and eroticism, precisely because the child was born not as a result of the life-giving powers of nature, but as a result of God's power over the natural. The Old Testament God manipulated the power of reproduction when he caused a woman of 90 to become pregnant. In some passages the name Isaac is connected with a word for laughter – ṣḥq – which sometimes has the meaning 'have sexual fun' (Genesis 21: 9–10, 26: 8) (Brenner 1990: 51–2, Stetkevych 1996: 33). With the birth of Isaac and the pun probably intended in the saying 'God has made laughter for me' (Genesis 21: 7), it seems that Jahweh has made a sexual joke directed against the old fertility cults with their potent women and erotic laughter.

Generally in the Old Testament, laughter had lost its playful connotations.[13] Even small children were not spared; short work was made of the children that laughed at or mocked the prophet Elisha, for instance. The prophet cursed them in the name of his god and two she-bears immediately came out of the wood and tore forty-two of the children asunder. The cruel punishment reflected the gravity of the crime and showed that it did not pay to mock the god of Israel (2 Kings 2: 23–4). Jahweh's superiority must not be challenged.

Though it seems that Jahweh's fierce laughter was a disembodied force, Jahweh's laughter had bodily connotations as well. These bodily connotations are seen, for instance, in Psalm 37, when God's laughter is contrasted with the wicked's gnashing of teeth, and in Psalm 59, where God's laughter opposes the heathens who bark like dogs, belch and have swords in their lips. These images of biting mouths and piercing teeth put derisive laughter in a revealing context. Divine laughter was a destructive force, it came from a wide open mouth, more powerful and terrible than those set with teeth and swords, ready to swallow and destroy. The bodily connotations of this laughter were opposite to those of the erotic laughter, which was associated with a body which opens itself up and produces. The image of the wide open mouth is found in different Hebrew expressions in the Bible which perhaps indicate derisive laughter; as one scholar put it, 'all seem to refer to the widening of the mouth in the mocking gesture of victorious laughter' (Brenner 1990: 57).[14]

Compared to the laughter of the Mesopotamian Anu, Jahweh's laughter was far more destructive. Anu's laughter put Adapa in his place and restored the cosmological balance which had been temporarily disturbed. Jahweh's laughter crushed and destroyed those who opposed him. This difference may be due in part to the fact that the historical context of Jahweh's divine laughter was different from that of the gods in Mesopotamia and Egypt. The fight of Jahweh's prophets on behalf of their god as well as for their own theological supremacy forms a background for Jahweh's laughter. This monotheistic emphasis is also connected with creation becoming a male prerogative carried out by means of God's creative word, with the assembly of gods and goddesses being banned from the cult, and with women no longer playing significant roles within the cult. Because of Jahweh's prophets' and theologians' attempts to destroy the fertility cults, erotic laughter was overruled. The prophets and priests of Jahweh carried out a religious revolution when they made their god the object of a monotheistic and moral cult (Garbini 1988). In this context, it comes as no surprise that they used mockery as a weapon.

DIVINE LAUGHTER: ITS CHANNELS AND CONSEQUENCES

Perhaps suprisingly, the laughter in the myths we have examined is not primarily playful and humorous. Rather, it is purposeful, often acting as a catalyst or underlining what has already happened.

We have examined two main types of laughter, the laughter of regeneration and the laughter of derision. These are both bodily. They draw their nourishment from either a symbolic context of sexuality and birth and a body which opens itself up in an act of creation, or from a context of destruction, biting and swallowing with a mouth set with swords. Those bodily contexts are dramatic and arouse emotions. They accentuate that it is within the power of laughter to be a direct channel of emotions – be it feelings of lust or of glory and power.

The consequences of divine laughter are far-reaching. The divine laughter characterizes the relationship between humans, gods and the world. Its space is the cosmos. This laughter is instrumental in preserving the divine/human hierarchy, putting humans in their place in relation to divine beings, making order in the world. In short, divine laughter appears as a mechanism of control that contributes to a rational management of the cosmos. The combination of laughter's eruptive quality, its anchoring in emotions, and its use as an instrument to enforce social and moral order is a powerful one. This rich connection between the emotional and bodily on the one hand and the rational and cosmological on the other is exploited when laughter is used as a symbol in Near Eastern myths and rituals. Social hierarchy, power and the management of the world are thus given emotional impetus, while the emotional is refined, and in the main, not allowed to get out of hand.

So far we have learnt that when laughter is preserved in texts, either as part of myths or in rituals, a balance is usually made between its inherent explosiveness and its purposeful exploitation. When, in the Near Eastern mythology, divine laughter is used in a purposeful way, its contact with the irrational is kept under control. But that control could also slip. As we move to the Greek sources, we see that laughter's aspect as a vehicle for the unthought and a force that transcends the limits of culture and society becomes prominent and alarming.

2

GREECE

When laughter touches the unthought

The symbol of laughter (*geloion*) in a religious context is more visible in Ancient Greece than in the ancient cultures of the Near East.[1] This is partly due to better source material, but laughter in Greece was also a primary medium for religious expression, even a god in its own right.[2] Laughter was part of cultic life. It was part of the theatre, where different aspects of the laughter culture were taken up by the dramatic genres and played out in honour of Dionysos. In festivals and comedies, laughter was utilized in the interest of the *polis*.

That Greek laughter was comic goes without saying. That it was also tragic has recently received more attention (Dillon 1991, Halliwell 1991, Meltzer 1990). The laughter cultivated in Greek comedies was playful. Social tensions could be vented, and through laughter, transformed into joy. The hero of the Greek comedy was the jester who for fun's sake played the role of the victim to amuse himself and others. This laughter existed within the framework of ritual in several of the festivals, in the *komos*, the comedies, the satyr-plays and the *symposion*.[3] A significant part of the comic element relied on erotic forms, usually of a religious origin. In the Near Eastern material, we find erotic laughter in connection with the goddesses' naked bodies. In Greece, the goddesses and their worshippers were joined by male figures as well.

The tragic laughter of Greece was born out of mockery, gave birth to shame and was an extension and intensification of derisive laughter.[4] Painful and never funny, it contributed to the sanction of ethical norms and was a motivating force in Greek culture. It received its most refined literary expression in the tragedies, but appears in the epics as well.[5] Tragic laughter – devoid of humour – generates fear. The derisive laughter of Jahweh was related to tragic

28

laughter, but Greek tragic laughter was aimed at specific victims and not, as Jahweh's laughter was, at foes and antagonists as a group. In Greece, tragic laughter's first purpose was its use as an efficient sanction against shameful behaviour, while Jahweh's laughter first of all reflected the fight for theological supremacy.

Lastly, laughter in Greece had aspects that made it more ambiguous and alarming than was immediately evident. Uncontrolled laughter seems to have been a source of anxiety, particularly for those philosophers who later tried to restrict laughter. When laughter expresses a transcending religious experience, which is neither fully explicable nor necessarily generally acceptable, it appears as a channel to the divine. In the cult and mythology of Dionysos, there are examples of how laughter expressed a transcendent religious experience, and of how it sometimes escaped socially accepted forms. But laughter's use as a characteristic of the divine is not restricted to Dionysos. The earliest examples of such use are found in the works of Hesiod and Homer.

CUNNING GODS/IMMORTAL GODS

Most religions reflect a belief in something fundamental that divides human existence from the divine, something that humans try to grasp in spite of God's prohibition. In Mesopotamia, Israel and Greece, humankind tried to attain a carefree existence and/or immortality, but was denied both. The relationship between humans and gods, as Hesiod describes it, was antagonistic, reflecting the fact that gods and humans were allotted different fates in the world: the gods were immortal, humans were not. The gods could live without toil, humans had to labour hard to get their food. This is the background of the battle of cunning and trickery between Zeus and the titan Prometheus, a duel accompanied by laughter and smiling. According to two complementary and interlocking passages in the *Theogony* and, the *Works and Days* (Vernant 1990a), Prometheus cheated Zeus over a sacrifice. The titan divided the meat of an ox in two portions, in the one he had put all the best meat, covered by the stomach, in the other he had put the white bones, but coated them with a thin layer of glistening fat.[6] The father of the gods judged by appearance and was fooled.[7] When Prometheus tricked Zeus, he did it smiling: 'But crooked-scheming Prometheus answered him [Zeus], smiling gently and intent on deceit' (*Theogony*, 546–7).

Prometheus is characterized throughout by his cunning

intelligence and his skill in trickery. His smile expresses those qualities. When Zeus hid fire from men, Prometheus stole it. Hesiod decribes Zeus' rage and the price man had to pay for his theft. Zeus set the gods to create a woman with the promising name Pandora, 'allgift', but this gift meant trouble (Songe Möller 1990):

> Son of Iapetos, clever above all others, you are glad at having stolen fire and outwitted me – a great calamity both for you yourself and for men to come. To set against the fire I shall visit them with an affliction in which they will all delight as they embrace their own destruction.
>
> So saying, the father of men and gods laughed out loud.
>
> (*Works and Days*, 54–9)

Zeus' revenge was marked by his divine laughter, which outdid Prometheus' deceitful smile.[8] This derisive laughter marks the turning point of the myth where the balance between Zeus and Prometheus, god and man, is finally shifted. It is the vindictive laughter of one who has been outwitted and is intent on having his revenge. We are reminded of the laughter of Anu when Adapa was tricked out of immortality. Adapa, however, never seems to have represented a real threat to Anu's power, as Prometheus represents to Zeus. While Adapa just had bad luck, Prometheus deliberately tried to outwit the father of the gods and did indeed obtain some benefits for which it had been worth fighting. In the story of Prometheus, laughter was part of a duel of cunning and trickery in a play for power.

In Homer's works, laughing gods are stock in trade, laughter being one of the gods' prerogatives and a symbol of their immortality (Friedländer 1934, Lesky 1961). Their boisterous, high-spirited belly laughter has given origin to the expression 'Homeric laughter'. At first glance, laughter in the *Iliad* and the *Odyssey* seems to be the opposite of tragic laughter: a joyful expression of the comic mode. But this impression is wrong; the very idea of a hearty, good-natured 'Homeric laughter' is deceptive. There are many comic elements in Homer, but the laughter of the *Iliad* and the *Odyssey* is never innocent; even the most comic situation is not without spite. These malicious undertones give the ludicrous a specific resonance (Meltzer 1990: 280). Much of what is comic in these epics is cruel because suffering and misfortune elicit laughter: the gods laugh at the crippled Hephaistos; Zeus laughs when Hera slaps Artemis' ears; Athena laughs when she fells Ares; prince Paris laughs when he wounds Diomedes; the Greeks laugh when Ajax falls in dung.

The two most famous examples of laughter in the world of gods are found in the *Iliad* (I, 570–611) and in the *Odyssey* (VIII, 266–369). The laughter is triggered both times by Hephaistos – in the *Iliad* when he appears as a clownish cupbearer and in the *Odyssey* when he catches Aphrodite and Ares in adultery.

In the *Iliad*, Homer made the assembly of the gods magnificent. They lived abundantly on Olympus and therefore in stark contrast to humans, but they were always in close contact with happenings on earth. When the *Iliad* starts, the war against Troy has raged for several years. The gods have favourites in both camps. Zeus has just promised to help the Trojans. His wife is furious and criticizes his decision. The father of the gods does not tolerate opposition in his own ranks and threatens to silence her. Then the situation is changed by a joke.

Hephaistos, the smith, limps forward. He makes the most artful things with his hands, but is crippled. Now he amuses the gods, and especially Zeus, with his account of how Zeus had taken him by his legs and thrown him down from Olympus because Hephaistos had intervened in a quarrel between Hera and Zeus. All day he fell until he landed half dead on Lemnos. After finishing his story, Hephaistos passes the cup to Hera and limps around the table to serve the other gods. The spectacle of this ungraceful, self-appointed cupbearer makes the gods dissolve in laughter, even Hera smiles, and the gods continue their feast until dawn.

What was so funny? Hephaistos made a fool of himself and made the others laugh at him. His act was a creative improvization, which has been likened to the role played by the *akletoi*, the professional entertainers at a symposion (Fehr 1990). Part of his success is explained by Hephaistos' parody of the gracious and beautiful Ganymede. In his imitation of Ganymede and by playing on his physical disabilities, Hephaistos exploits his handicap with great comic profit. The laughter of the gods was not only at Hephaistos, but also with him, at the same time as it stressed the great distance between Zeus and the other gods. Their merriment does not challenge Zeus. On the contrary, Hephaistos confirmed Zeus' role as ruler, and was himself a living illustration of the consequences for those who dared to oppose the ruling god. In this case, laughter supported the hierarchy of power between the ruler and those he ruled over and created a spirit of community among the gods.

Laughter could also be used to mark distance from a victim. In this case, the victim is virtually laughed down. In the eighth song of the *Odyssey* (266–369), the minstrel Demodocus sings about divine adultery with ludicrous consequences (Burkert 1960, C. G. Brown 1989, Hart 1943). The poem tells the tale about what happened when Aphrodite deceived her husband, Hephaistos, with Ares. The cunning smith set a trap for the couple, making an artificial net and hiding it over their bed. Animated by lust the two lovers hurried to bed, hearing and seeing nothing before the net fell down and held them firmly, unable to move a limb. The roars and shouts of Hephaistos when he found them summoned the other gods to see a ludicrous spectacle. Their reaction was one of boisterous hilarity, 'unquenchable laughter arose among the blessed gods as they saw the craft of wise Hephaestus' (*Odyssey*, 236–7).

The song culminates with the gods joking and enjoying themselves immensely – Hermes confides to Apollo that he would have liked to have changed places with Ares, even if it meant being made a public spectacle. This makes the gods laugh even more, before Hephaistos is persuaded by Poseidon to let the lovers loose and they flee in opposite directions.

In this archaic case of adultery Hephaistos subjected the unfortunate couple to merciless laughter by his use of cunning and skill. That was his revenge, but it is doubtful if this made Hephaistos, the cuckold, less ludicrous. The laughter of the gods was mocking, mirroring a society where public ridicule was used for ethical sanctions and social control. But even as the laughter of the gods reflected the norms of Greek society, it also set the gods apart from human beings and underscored their divinity and immortality (Burkert 1960: 140). In this case, though the divine adulterers were shamed and their shame made immortal, their adultery had no further consequences. In the human world, it would have been different. Adulterers received a severe punishment and could even be killed.

Laughter was not marginal in the Greek conception of their gods. Considering how it surfaces again and again in the context of myths and ritual, it must rather be seen as a defining characteristic of the divine world. The songs of the *Iliad* and the *Odyssey* were sung by travelling bards in the courts of princes and among common people, and they were later memorized in the schools. People laughed at the exalted gods, at the crippled Hephaistos and at the amorous Aphrodite and her fierce lover. The gods had laughed first: all of Olympus roared with laughter at Hephaistos' performance, and at least the males among them showed uninhibited delight at the torments of the lovers and the agony of the cuckold. Human laughter was mixed with that of the divine, demonstrating that it was permissible to laugh at the gods. However, the last laugh is always the best laugh. The ultimate laughter belonged to the gods, standing as a sign of their power. Both in Hesiod and in Homer, divine laughter exists in a context of cunning skill and male power, either as part of a struggle for supremacy or as a demonstration of supremacy. These myths of divine laughter are very similar to the myths of Anu and Adapa and of Anu and Kumarbi. All of the myths reek of lust for power and domination, and in each of them laughter contributes to keeping society stable and 'normal'.

In the first song of the *Iliad* the laughter of the gods resolved a conflict and developed into the laughter of the *symposion* where community was restored. However, the laughter was triggered by a joker who cunningly turned the laughter against himself. In the eighth song of the *Odyssey*, the laughter is one of derision and shame, but set within an erotic frame.

LAUGHING WOMEN

The erotic face of Near Eastern religious laughter is also found in Greece, where it was rather prominent and often connected with the power of women.

Greek erotic laughter was not restricted to the confines of narrative and mythological fiction; it also seeped into the world of humans and into their rituals. Ritual abuse, jesting and obscene language – *aischrologia* – played a role in all the female festivals for the goddess Demeter (Thesmophoria, Stenia and Haloa) as well as in the Eleusinia (where men also participated). Another important goddess, Aphrodite, was called 'genial', a pun on *philommedes* and *philomeides*, 'genital-loving' and 'laughter-loving' (Zaidman and Pantel 1992: 153). Hilarity and laughter were a part of her worship, especially in the festival of the Adonia (Winkler 1990: 188–209, Detienne 1977).

The mysteries in Eleusis took place in the autumn month Boedromion (September/October) and lasted for one week. According to the Homeric hymn to Demeter, Hades had abducted Kore, Demeter's daughter, and the sorrowful goddess searched everywhere for her child. At last she came to Eleusis and sat down, veiled and in mourning, neither drinking nor eating, responding to no one. Because of Demeter's sorrow, life withered away on earth. Not until the servant-girl Iambe took recourse to jokes and mockery did the unsmiling goddess start to laugh:

> Unsmiling tasting neither food nor drink,
> she sat wasting with desire for her deep-girt daughter,
> until knowing Iambe jested with her and
> mocking with many a joke moved the holy goddess
> to smile and laugh and keep a gracious heart –
> Iambe, who later pleased her moods as well.
>
> (*The Homeric Hymn to Demeter*, 200–5, Foley 1994: 12)

What is Iambe joking about? The hymn does not tell. In addition to the general obligation to say nothing about the secret parts of the mysteries, the hymn's author(s) may also have wanted to spare the audience embarrassment (Foley 1994: 175–8). For the servant girl Iambe was not merely one who jokes coarsely, she was the incarnation of ritual jokes of an indecent character, Iambe being the name of one genre in Greek poetry used in jesting verses (West 1974). Iambe's role in the Homeric Demeter hymn is, in other versions of the myth, played by a character named Baubo (Olender 1990). Baubo's name means 'vagina'. She is sculptured in terracotta figures found at the sanctuary of Demeter and Kore at Priene, with a face which goes directly over her private parts and legs, becoming simultaneously a laughing face and female genitals (Olender 1990). Clement of Alexandria tells us that it was Baubo, not Iambe, who managed to get the mourning Demeter to laugh. He describes how Baubo is offended because Demeter will not accept the drink she has prepared. But when Baubo uncovers her genitals and exhibits them to the goddess, perhaps playing with them and making her lower abdomen resemble the child Iacchus, the spectacle delights the goddess so much that she accepts the draught. Clement quotes an Orphic verse:

> This said, she drew aside her robes, and showed
> A sight of shame; child Iacchus was there,
> And laughing, plunged his hand below her breasts.
> Then smiled the goddess, in her heart she smiled,
> And drank the draught from out the glancing cup.[9]
>
> (*The Exhortation to the Greeeks*, 2, 21)

In this Orphic verse quoted by Clement the exposure of the female body – with its double aspects of erotic power and generative functions – got the mourning goddess to laugh. As in the Egyptian myth where Hathor exposed herself to Re, the laughter in the Demeter myth occurs in a situation where destruction reigns. Then the exhibition of the naked female body relieves the tension. And even if Iambe had not displayed her body, her obscene joking has a similar function. In the poetic use of the myth, Iambe is referred to as *athyroisin*, 'doorless', and in a hymn to Demeter composed by the poet Philikos (third century BC), Iambe says to Demeter, 'If you are willing to loosen the bonds of your mourning, I can set you free'. Both expressions stress Iambe's function, which is to open up that which is closed (Olender 1990: 85–6, 105). The ritual drink, *kykeon*, which Demeter drank, further contributes to this interpretation. The drink was made of barley, water and pennyroyal (*glechon*). Pennyroyal is a herb which stimulates uterine contractions and in antiquity was recommended for use in the delivery chamber (Scarborough 1991). In the Old Comedy it was linked specifically to female sexuality, but also to digestive problems (Foley 1994: 47). A general function of this drink seems to have been to clear passages for a new beginning and for life to flow. Once again, then, laughter stands in a context of an opening up of the female body.

The episode of Iambe/Baubo is the turning point of the myth. Demeter, who was *agelastos*, 'without laughter' (in other versions of the myth, she is sitting by the Agelastos Petra, 'the rock without laughter') (Apollodorus, *The Library*, I, v, i) laughs and again busies herself with the tasks of life most fitting for a goddess of motherhood and fertility – child-care and the care of nature.[10]

The theme of shameful jokes and obscene language was also part of Greek rituals. On their way from Athen to Eleusis to be initiated in the mysteries, when they passed a certain bridge, the *mystes* were met by veiled or masked persons, *gephyristai*, who uttered insults at them and made obscene gestures. On the night after their arrival, the women sang and danced and used obscene language. The use of jokes and obscene language with the purpose of making the participants laugh seems to have been essential in the cult of Demeter, being reported at all her important festivals.

The most widespread of these festivals was the Thesmophoria, which was held everywhere in the Greek world, and in which only women participated.[11] It was no female club or sewing circle, but a festival of the state where the women carried out the old rites on behalf of the *polis*, and where they had female rulers and a female council.[12] The festival had been preceded by the Stenia, a celebration of the return of Demeter, including a night of ribald jesting. In Athens, the festival started with the day of ascent (*anodos*), continued with the day of fasting (*nesteia*) and ended with a day of 'Fair Off-spring' (*kalligeneia*). During the feast, possibly on the second day, the women took up decaying remains of piglets that had earlier been thrown into trenches together with cakes shaped as serpents and genitals. The ingredients were mixed with seed-corn, put on the altar and afterwards scattered on the fields. The women had ribald fun with each other and indulged in indecent language and obscenities. The word for 'piglet' (*choeros*), for instance, was a usual stand-in for female genitals. According to one source, the obscene language originated in Iambe's joking with Demeter (Apollodorus, *The Library*, I, v, i).

The laughter and indecent joking seem related to the ruling themes of the festival: sexuality and fertility. Laughter symbolized the bodily opening up. The theme of opening up is also expressed through the plants used for building beds and huts for the women: they were medical herbs with various gynaecological functions such as opening the uterus (menstruation, abortion, birth), stimulating milk production and obstructing conception. Some of them were symbols of fertility (Dahl 1976: 45–51). Classical authors mention that the plants were used to keep snakes away and to guard the chastity of the women. Rather puzzling for modern critics is that the symbols used seem to give contradictory messages; they have con-notations of fertility as well as working against it (Versnel 1993). One answer to this apparent riddle could be that at the same time as the fertility of women was promoted, it also had to be held in check. Fertility was exploited to a ritual end, but was not allowed to go beyond certain limits.

Another possible answer is that it was in the women's own inter-est to boost their powers of fertility and to keep these powers under their own control (Nixon 1995). Thus, it was within the power and choice of women to decide whether or not to generate. (Remember how Demeter withheld her power and rendered the earth sterile when Kore was abducted by Hades.) If this is the case, then anti-fertility and contraceptive drugs are not out of place, but must rather be seen as natural and obvious ingredients in women's rituals. While women's joking and women's laughter at the Thesmophoria clearly represented an opening up to the forces of life, they also show that these women intended to keep those forces in the firm grip of their own control. In line with this interpretation, we are, perhaps, not only listening to the echoes of 'the laughter of the oppressed', but also to the laughter of women who were knowing and powerful.[13]

The obscene joking may have been a substitute activity for more direct sexual practices, in the same manner as the mouth and the eating of cakes shaped as genitals may be seen as replacing the female genitals and the sexual act (Zeitlin 1982: 144). Because ritualized comments on sex and on the polarities of the sexes were natural in these festivals, part of the women's fun could have been mockery aimed directly at men. As Winkler put it, when women control the mysteries of life 'phallic men are peripheral and their pretensions amusing' (Winkler 1990: 206). But more importantly, obscene joking is a sort of cultural creativity in which the jokers exploit the powers inherent in laughter. Demeter's mythology is here and elsewhere connected with women's procreativity, associating it with the fertility of the fields and the crop and the blessing of offspring. The focus of the feast was on female sexuality and procreation; the laughter of the women in the service of Demeter was regenerative for them and for their society.

BETWEEN COMEDY AND TRAGEDY

Even if coarse joking and erotic laughter were typical for some of the female cults in Greece, they were not restricted to the goddesses and their cults. The god of laughter was Dionysos. Beside the mythology of Hesiod and Homer and the cult of Demeter, Dionysos' cult is the third great context of religious laughter in ancient Greece. Not only regenerative laughter of the erotic and comic variety, but also derisive and tragic laughter found their special forms in his cult (Henrichs 1982). His most important symbol was a phallus, carried in his processions. When the phallus was prominent in the feasts of the god, it was accompanied by much joy and coarse joking. It is true that he had cults where women were the principal participants, but he also presided over the masculine *komos*. Dionysos is at the root of the three dramatic genres: the satyric drama; the comedies; and the tragedies.[14]

Satyrs were drawn early into the company of Dionysos. The satyric dramas featured them, clad in a loin-cloth with a horse tail and a phallus. Their mythological prototypes were hybrids of men and animals, a muddling of the categories of man and beast typical for Greece.[15] Vital, unrestrained and greedy, they danced wildly, were heavy drinkers and were clearly male, ready to spring on all women who came their way. On vase paintings they masturbate without inhibitions, facing toward the spectators (Lissarrague 1990).

The satyrs were the only figures in Greek art who really laughed. They laughed uproariously so that their teeth were visible (Brunnsåker 1976). This laughter is in keeping with their entire being: they opened themselves up to the world and helped themselves to everything it had to offer. They were without inhibitions and their appetites were without bounds. Compared with female erotic characters, such as Baubo, and obscene female joking at the festivals, the satyrs give the impression of being monstrous forms focused on fun. They do not seem to exploit the powers of laughter for a 'serious' end as the female forms seem to have done. This is almost certainly due to the different roles of men and women in Greece. In a patriarchal society where women's lives were very constricted, the exposure of women was a dramatic break with common decency and had therefore great ritual power.

The ritualization of laughter in Greece found its lasting expression in the genre of comedy, organized in Athens from the beginning of the fifth century. The year 405 BC saw the first performance of the most famous comedy of them all, *Frogs*, written by Aristophanes.[16]

Frogs is full of whims and inventions. What sort of god does Aristophanes introduce us to? His Dionysos has at best a caricature's likeness to the original. In Aristophanes' version of the god the force which so frequently made this god dangerous is hidden. In *Frogs*, Dionysos has become human. He talks nonsense, yet combines the stupidities of the fool with wit. When the play starts Dionysos is dressed up as the demigod and hero Heracles. Together with the slave Xanthias he travels to the Underworld to bring back Euripides, who has recently died. Dionysos crosses the Styx where he has a croaking match with the frogs, and wins. The god is mortally afraid of what he is going to meet on the other side. Suddenly he directs himself to his own priest in the front row of the theatre: 'My priest, protect me, and we'll sup together' (297). The doorkeeper of Hades mistakes Dionysos for the real Heracles who once stole the terrible Cerberus. He threatens Dionysos, who dirties his pants, sinks on his knees and exclaims, 'I've done it: call the god', an irreverent play on a ritual formula from the Eleusinian mysteries (479). The play continues in a similar vein.

How shall we interpret this sort of joking? Did Aristophanes do his best to undermine religious tradition? Did he mock the sacred and make a fool of Dionysos because this master of comedy was an apostate in his heart? Or was it the other way around: were the gods still sacred and religion a serious business, with comedies and carnivals being a way to escape the burden of religion? Both these explanations assume a sharp division between the sacred and the profane. But *Frogs* is a witness to the lack of such a division. The play was staged on the festival days of the god in the presence of his statue and his priest.

If these explanations are too simple, there may be more complicated ones: the purpose of mocking the sacred may have been to show that the gods of the myths were made by humans and that their reality transcended human conceptions of them. To mock the gods was to mock human ideas of the gods. The gods stood over their own crude anthropomorphic representations and were not struck by their jokes. But this explanation does not quite hit the mark, either. It reduces the laughter which the play evoked to a mere pedagogical tool, and it reduces the divinity of Dionysos. We must not forget that even if Dionysos was cast as ludicrous in *Frogs*, he was, as a comic hero, the one who played the main role and commanded the stage throughout the play. A more likely explanation may be that one of the moods of the divinity of Dionysos was precisely unrestrained laughter. Through laughter people were lifted out of their day-to-day troubles into a happy union with their god. In other words, laughter was the medium through which Dionysos expressed his divinity and by which he drew his adherents to him.

In *Frogs*, Dionysos revealed himself at his most human – a clown, a coward and a jabbering fool. In short, he took the lead and made his people follow him in glorious laughter, as was seemly for 'the god of laughter'. However, just as easily as Dionysos could sweep his adherents with him in a divine laughter, he could also sweep them up in divine madness. Even in this madness, laughter thrived. The comic could turn out to be tragic; the tragic could be comic. That which amused the god did not necessarily amuse men.

Dionysos was a dangerous god. He is often represented as drunk with vine leaves around his head. But alcoholic intoxication was only one layer of his cult. Those who worshipped him were also intoxicated by ecstasy and madness. Wine could trigger it off, but Dionysiac intoxication was aroused by deeper forces as well.

Dionysos' official side was cultivated by the Athenians: among them he transgressed the boundaries, but within limits. In the ecstatic cults, however, the adherents of Dionysos experienced the god's presence and an immediate contact with him. In Dionysos' service, one's personal identity disappeared; the boundary between his worshippers and the god was wiped away. His worshippers would, in Dionysiac madness, swarm over the countryside, tearing to pieces what they met on their way and devouring it. The dark power of Dionysos, inexplicable and sacred, threatened to spring forth and destroy everything in its way.

What happens when laughter is directly brought in contact with the darker aspects of Dionysos? In the tragedy, *Bacchae* (written by Euripides and staged in the same year as *Frogs*, the year after Euripides died), Dionysos is again on the stage, but with a completely different and sinister mask.[17]

In *Bacchae*, King Pentheus, the ruler of Thebes, has decided that Dionysos is not to be worshipped in the city because Dionysos oversteps the limits of decency and drives his adherents mad. Pentheus mocks the god's adherents and describes them as ridiculous. He even laughs at the god scornfully (248–53, 272, 322). Because of Pentheus' blasphemy, Dionysos wants to demonstrate his divinity to Thebes. The god comes in disguise and tricks Pentheus into putting on women's clothes and spying on the maenads. The god leads Pentheus away in female attire through the city, and thus makes him a laughingstock in front of his people. On the pretext that Pentheus should get a better view of the wild play of the maenads, without himself being seen, Dionysos makes him climb a tree. The god promises the king that he will return 'In your mother's arms' (968). Visible to everyone Pentheus takes his seat in the tree. Immediately Dionysos points him out to the flock of the maenads and shouts to them: 'I bring the one who makes you and me and my mystic rites a mockery; but take revenge on him' (1080–1).

The maenads tear Pentheus down from the tree. Agave, his own mother, is in the lead. Pentheus beseeches her to spare his life, but the women are insane. They tear him to pieces, limb from limb. According to the chorus Dionysos is smiling: 'Go, o Bacchus, beast, with laughing face throw around the hunters of bacchants the deadly noose as he falls under the herd of maenads' (1020-3). Agave carries her son's head in triumph upon her thyrsus-point back to Thebes. In this gruesome way the promise of the god is fulfilled; Pentheus is carried in his mother's arms into Thebes. His mother thinks she is carrying the head of a lion.

Dionysos tricks everyone into participating in his mortal

masquerade and stages a divine joke which ends with the death of Pentheus. Pentheus falls into the clutches of the laughing god and suffers a terrible death. The actor who played the god probably carried a smiling mask, and it is mentioned three times that the god laughs (380, 439, 1021).[18] But surely, the laughter was disturbing, signalling how the tragic and the comic merge in the figure of Dionysos. *Bacchae* is comedy and tragedy at the same time, depending on whether it is seen from the point of view of the divine hero or of his human victim. While the audience laughed at Dionysos in *Frogs*, Dionysos laughs at human beings in *Bacchae*. The divine joke is cruel and destroys its object. Seen together, the Euripidean and the Aristophanian Dionysos show us the dynamics in the Athenian conception of divine laughter as it appeared in the theatre.

CHAOTIC LAUGHTER

One more aspect of the Dionysian laughter must be commented upon – its chaotic dimension. The laughter of Dionysos points to a dimension beyond normal human thought and experience. It is a laughter which is disruptive and unpredictable. Such a chaotic laughter is found in other gods as well.

For instance, the laughter of the goat-herd god Pan could be humorous and express fertility and joy, but it could also be disturbing, causing panic. As with Dionysos, so also with Pan: categories are confused; there is a blending of human and animal, an intermingling of sexuality and fear (Borgeaud 1995). Pan could also possess his adherents, and maniacal laughter was probably the main symptom of this Pan-ic possession (*panoleptos*) (Borgeaud 1988: 107–8, 139). Pan's mythical connections were to the rural, but, as we saw with Dionysos in *Bacchae*, the divine laughter of chaos might also erupt in the middle of the *polis*. According to Suetonius, when Emperor Caligula wanted to remove the magnificent statue of Zeus in Olympia, made by Pheidias 450 years earlier, and take it to Rome, the statue 'suddenly emitted such a cackle of laughter that the scaffolding collapsed and the workmen fled' (Suetonius, *The Lives of the Caesars*, Gaius Caligula, 57). The incident is interpreted as one of a string of bad omens predicting the death of the emperor.

The smiling mask of Dionysos is a theatrical prop of *Bacchae*; the laughter of Pan is heard in the midst of nature; the statue of Zeus cackles within the temple. Thus, the chaotic laughter is found in different types of sources and in various contexts. Yet, common to all its expressions is the laughter's unexpected and ominous nature. This divine laughter made human beings tremble with fear, both repelling them and fascinating them at the same time.[19] This laughter was not instrumental for human purposes; on the contrary, it was an eruption of the divine in the middle of the world. Strange and inexplicable, it opened up a channel into the chaotic dimensions of being. Given the chaotic potential of Greek laughter it is perhaps not surprising that from within the rich laughter culture of Greece, voices were raised in favour of keeping laughter strictly under control.

3

ROME

Critic of laughter and critical laughter

So far we have seen laughter as a genuine religious expression, blossoming in myths and rituals, a characteristic of the divine. It established connections between humans and gods, individuals and society, the body and the world. In the Ancient Near Eastern and Greek worlds we have examined thus far, the power of laughter is unquestionable. Because of that power, Greek philosophers strove to put laughter in the firm grip of rational control. Theirs was a new attitude towards laughter – that of investigation, scepticism and criticism. The classicist Bracht Branham is probably right when he says that 'there seems to have been an important shift in Greek thinking about laughter and the comic in the fourth century' (Branham 1989: 52). The philosophers were not sympathetic to laughter, but by singling laughter out as a subject for interest, its critics bore out the general impression that laughter in Greek culture was loud and important, a force in its own right. The philosophers, on their side, wanted to remove it from its privileged position and subordinate it to more serious issues.

'The earlier dramatists found their fun in obscenity, the moderns prefer innuendo, which marks a great advance in decorum' (*Nicomachean Ethics*, IV, 8, 6). These words by Aristotle reveal that he did not appreciate either laughter's inclination to overstep boundaries or its delight in indecencies, and thus distrusted the consequences of uninhibited laughter. He saw improper laughter as a threat to self-control. To Aristotle, people laughed and joked too much. He criticized those who went to extremes when they joked. Humour with moderation was the point. His distinction between *liberal* and *illiberal* – good-natured and ill-natured – jests came to characterize the thinking about humour for centuries to come (Grant 1924). The difference between the two is a question of

43

frequency, language and impact on the audience. One should joke moderately, consider the audience, never lapse into vulgarities and never deliberately hurt anyone. Plato had gone further: ideally, harmful laughter should be forbidden (*Laws*, 935–6). No worthy person must ever be represented as overcome with laughter, least of all the gods (*Republic*, 388e).

Hand in hand with this palpable eagerness to restrict and regulate laughter went a certain curiosity. Both Plato and Aristotle speculated about why people laughed and what constituted the comic. In the dialogue *Philebus*, Plato presents the ridiculous (*geloion*) as a kind of vice (*Philebus*, 48–50). According to Plato, laughter represented ignorance. His point was that anyone who ridiculed anything – with the exception of stupidity and vice – was stupid, because such a person possessed the opposite attitude of the Delphic ideal, self-knowledge (de Vries 1985). Aristotle stressed the feeling of superiority on the part of the one who laughs. He classified laughter as part of the ugly, a form of defect or deformity which, however, is not harmful to anyone else. As an example he took the comic mask, which is ugly and distorted but not painful.[1]

Though philosophers such as Aristotle and Plato were pioneers in the study of laughter, they also turned laughter into a trivial thing. In their efforts to quench laughter's violence and impropriety, they failed to appreciate that genuine laughter is without morals and that it could be an apt expression of a transcendent religious experience.

Though the influence of the philosophers is difficult to measure precisely, the critique of laughter, especially that found in Aristotle, was clearly continued by Greek philosophers such as Theophrastus, Demetrius, Plutarch and some of the Stoics, and further developed by Roman philosophers and authors (Grant 1924: 142).

'ALL THIS BUSINESS OF LAUGHTER-RAISING IS TRIVIAL'[2]

Like their Greek colleagues, the Romans considered laughter within a context of rationality. Rationality prefers orderliness and useful-ness; one should not lose control over oneself. It was only by making itself useful and by not challenging the general order that laughter could be accepted and made respectable. For even if they wanted to restrict laughter and regarded it as a trivial thing, the Greek and Roman philosophers also saw its utilitarian value (Arrobius, *Rhetoric*, 1419b; Aristotle, *Nicomachean Ethics*, IV, 8). Plato and Aristotle and their successors emphasized that a good laugh can revive the mind and thus could be of use as a preparation for more serious pursuits. Accordingly, rhetoric was one systematic context in which the use of laughter was developed. In works by Cicero and Quintilian, laughter, wit and humour are extensively commented upon (Cicero, *De Oratore*, II, 54–71; *Orator*, 26; *De Officiis*, I, 29–30; Quintilian, *Institutio Oratoria*, VI, 3). According to their view, laughter should be an instrument in the service of an orator, who, on his side, was advised to use laughter with care, consideration and, not the least, control:

> We here merely suggest that the orator should use ridicule with a care not to let it be too frequent lest it become buffoonery; nor ridicule of a smutty nature, lest it be that of low farce; nor pert, lest it be impudent; nor aimed at misfortune, lest it be brutal; nor at crime, lest laughter take the place of loathing; nor should the wit be inappropriate to his own character, to that of the jury, or to the occasion; for all these points come under the head of impropriety.
>
> (Cicero, *Orator*, 26, 88)

By classifying kinds of jokes and things laughable and by abundant quotes of jests made by their contemporaries or forefathers, the ancient rhetoricians demonstrated how to raise a laugh. The usefulness of laughter was that it prevented people from thinking a speech tedious; instead it helped them to absorb its message and take the side of the orator (*De Oratore*, II, 58, 236). In Greek and Roman works about laughter, it is emphasized that wit is like salt, it flavours the food, but should be used sparingly. In other words, the position of laughter should be subordinate. That does not mean that what was joked about was of marginal interest. If we take into consideration the conviction of Cicero 'that whatever subjects I may touch upon, as being sources of laughing-matters, may equally well, as a rule, be sources of serious thoughts' (*De Oratore*, II, 61, 248), and apply it to religion, it follows that what was singled out for scorn in religious matters may well reflect serious religious concerns of the Roman empire. So, in order to derive 'austere and serious thoughts' (*De Oratore*, II, 61, 250) from laughing matters we ask: what sort of religious themes were chosen as 'laughable' by pagan and Christian rhetoric in the Roman empire? What do these themes signify for the symbolic value of critical laughter? What characterizes this critical laughter in relation to the types of laughter we have already examined in Egypt, Mesopotamia and Greece?

CRITICAL LAUGHTER

To understand critical laughter, we must first see this type of laughter in its proper religio-historical setting, which was in a process of change.

In the second century BC, Greece lost her independence and became part of the Roman empire. In this new world, Greek and Roman gods developed side by side with gods from other cultures. The religious situation was characterized by plurality, tolerance and creativity. Old religions and new blossomed as never before in a peculiar cultural mixture that is sometimes called syncretism. The old gods had been confronted by divine immigrants like the Egyptian Isis, Cybele from Asia Minor and the Iranian Mithra. That these gods were supplements rather than alternatives to the Greek and Roman pantheon is shown, for instance, when Clea, a priestess of Apollon in Delphi, was also initiated into the rites of Egyptian Isis (Fox 1988: 184–5). The authorities wanted people to honour the traditional Greek and Roman gods, but usually did not prevent them from worshipping other gods as well.

In many ways, the Roman culture of late antiquity was a culture of pleasure. Laughter thrived. The festival days were many, rich in bread and circuses, and appropriately called *ludi*, 'games', which stressed their playful character (Huizinga 1970: 174). Everyone attended the Roman Games replete with gladiator fights, chariot races and bloodstained scenes. In the temples, scenes from mythology were acted out in a spectacular fashion with choir songs and musical performances, and no religious festival took place without dancing (MacMullen 1981: 20–5). For a short time the old world was turned upside down. In the feast of the Saturnalia in December, masters waited on their servants; in later periods the entire city was drawn into the Saturnalian festivities (Versnel 1993: 136–227). According to Seneca, the whole city went insane (*Epistle* 18). In the prospering theatres, Roman life was turned topsy-turvy. The most famous of the Roman playwrights, Plautus, mocked the gods most irreverently and parodied sacred practices. But Plautian laughter was also a holiday laughter. When the plays ended, it was back to 'the business of being Roman' (Segal 1987: 169).

In the Roman world, as in Greece and the Near East, laughter had traditionally been a symbol of regeneration and renewal. The feast of Saturnalia and the Plautian comedies were contexts for that type of laughter. Another example of laughter's regenerative associations

46

is the Lupercalia, the 'Feast of Wolves'. In this feast, the foreheads of two young men were touched with a bloodstained knife, then the stain was wiped off, and they were required to laugh. When they ran about afterwards almost naked, carrying a thong, young women did not try to avoid them, because they believed the blows from the thong promoted conception and easy childbirth (Plutarch, *Romulus*, 21). The rite may have started as a means to keep wolves away from the flocks of sheep; in later days, the feast and the laughter it evoked connoted fertility and new life, holding death and destruction at bay.

Regenerative laughter was also found in Roman literature, as in the much-loved novel of Apuleius from Madaurus in Africa, *The Golden Ass*. The novel's main actor, Lucius, is transformed into an ass by black magic. He is doomed to wander about as a donkey, and his experiences are both terrible and ridiculous – the book is full of sex and crime, horror and grotesques. In one episode, Lucius participates in a Festival of Laughter, 'the most welcome of the gods' (3, 11), and becomes the butt of a practical joke.[3] In this way Laughter is celebrated, and Lucius is inscribed as its patron. In another example – Virgil's famous *Fourth Eclogue* – a divine child will be born, a symbol of the return of the Golden Age when the earth will produce without agriculture, and the lions will no longer be dangerous (*Eclogue*, IV, 60–4). This child is encouraged to smile to his mother, for laughter is a symbol of regeneration and a new beginning (Norden 1924).

A new world had after all been born within the old; however, the regenerative laughter of the festivals, theatres and literature did not rule alone. It was joined by the critical laughter of religious plurality. In this new world, gods, religious conceptions and ritual practices were called into question, partly because they had become too numerous. The philosophers' doubt, the Church Fathers' scorn and the poets' mockery offer complementary critical descriptions of the exceedingly complex religious picture of these times. In a world where different religions meet, curiosity, surprise and intrigue, as well as horror and animosity all arise. Some of these feelings were ventilated through laughter. Juvenal remarks in one of his satires: 'Who ever sneered at the Gods in the days of old? Who would have dared to laugh at the earthenware bowls or black pots of Numa, or the brittle plates made out of Vatican clay?' (*Satire*, VI, 342–4). In Juvenal's time, he and other satirists made fun of what they conceived as the general superstitions of their contemporaries. The Roman Seneca and the Greek Plutarch mocked Judaic rituals, in

particular the Sabbath observations. The Christian Clement from
Alexandria and Tertullian from Carthage mocked pagan religions in
general. The African Apuleius made fun of the Syrian Goddess. The
Syrian Lucian laughed at everybody *except* the Syrian Goddess, about
whom he wrote a treatise (which perhaps he meant to be ironical)
(*De Dea Syria*). And virtually everybody ridiculed the Egyptian cults.
Satirists used critical laughter against other religions, but mockery
was also directed at elements in the satirists' own religions.

Critical laughter presupposes a changed perspective towards
religion. Up until Hellenistic times we have seen laughter as a
force within a religion, an integral part of myths and rituals.
Gradually laughter moved to the margins. Those who laughed
stood on the sideline, watching. They did not take part in what
they observed, at least not wholeheartedly, because they no longer
shared, or had never shared, the convictions of the participants.
The potential for cultural change lies in critical laughter. Such a
laughter was found in several of the literary genres of the day –
novels, diatribes, dialogues, satires and apologies. These genres
were testimonies to an educated class which questioned old traditions along with popular practices and new cults, and used critical
laughter to do so.

When religion is held up to ridicule, its symbols, ideas and practices are taken out of a sacred context. A statue loses its divinity and
becomes stone or wood; the loveplay of Ares and Aphrodite is
reduced to adultery; gods in animal shapes are regarded as mere
animals; divine beings become demons. By unexpected turns, by
caricature, irony and other rhetorical devices the religious is held up
to derision: see what you really are worshipping; how ridiculous it is!

As one example of the desacralizing effects of critical laughter,
we will concentrate on the satirical writings of Lucian. Lucian's
parodies and jests at the expense of the divine are representative of
the religious themes that were picked out for criticism in the early
Roman empire, and his writings offer us some fine examples of
critical laughter at work.

ON TOUR WITH THE GODS

Lucian was a Syrian who made an early career as a sophist and
rhetorician. He travelled widely in the Roman empire and was paid
for his public speaking. Lucian wrote comical parodies and satires
about nearly all aspects of classical culture – philosophy, poetry and

religion. History shows mixed feelings about Lucian. Even if he has been much read, earlier generations of classical scholars saw him as 'irresponsible' because of his rough treatment of the classical tradition (Branham 1989: 1–23). His contemporaries must have viewed him differently, though; he managed to make a living out of touring with his satirical dialogues in which he made fun of the gods, even if those dialogues never made his fortune. In his last years he had to take up a post in the service of the Emperor in Egypt.

Religion was one of Lucian's favourite subjects. He poked fun at old gods, new gods, oracles and men who passed for holy. Lucian's treatment of oracles is malicious and he shows genuine anger at one of the new prophets; he tells us that he bit the finger of the notorious Alexander of Abonoteichos when he pretended that he was going to kiss the prophet's hand.

One of the most ludicrous of Lucian's twenty-five *Dialogues of the Gods* is *The Assembly of the Gods*, which parodies the pantheon. In this miniature dialogue, Momos, the god of sarcasm, confronts Zeus about the state of Olympus: too many gods have been welcomed into the home of the gods.[4] Momos gives a hilarious survey of traditional gods, 'barbarian' gods, animal gods, heroes and some of the divine abstracts: Virtue, Nature, Destiny and Chance. Zeus promises Momos to appoint a commission that will investigate the different claims to divinity. No quarter will be given: 'For if anyone fails to provide this evidence, it won't matter a bit to the Comissioners that he has a large temple on earth and men think him a god' (*The Assembly of the Gods*, 19, in MacLeod 1991: 67). Momos has already had the audacity to suggest that in case gods do not pass the test, their cities should rather 'raise tombs in their honour and erect gravestones in place of their altars' (*ibid.*).[5]

In *Zeus: The Tragic Actor* the gods are summoned when a debate takes place on earth about the existence of the gods between the Epicurean Damis, an atheist, and the Stoic Timocles. Zeus is full of fear because he anticipates that the atheist Damis will win and the gods will lose their sacrifices. When it turns out that Damis actually is winning, Hermes consoles Zeus and says that the majority of the Greeks and all the barbarians still believe in the gods even if the philosophical dispute did not turn out in their favour. That was probably the case. It was not likely that the common person shared the outspoken scepticism of the philosophers, nor would their scepticism have been likely to alter fundamentally the commoner's beliefs. Lucian's dialogues show how alive the classical mythological tradition actually was, at the same time as they reveal how ludicrous this tradition was viewed to be by some.

Another topic of Lucian's jokes in *Zeus: The Tragic Actor*, was the flourishing oracle cults. Momos, the mouthpiece of Lucian, says bluntly to Apollo: 'in your oracles you are ambiguous and riddling and you unconcernedly toss most of them into debatable ground so that your hearers need another Apollo to interpret them' (*Zeus: The Tragic Actor*, 28, in Lucian, *Complete Works*). When Apollo really brings forth an oracle, Momos laughs himself to pieces and is corrected by Zeus: 'What are you guffawing about, Momos? Surely there is nothing to laugh at in the situation we are facing. Stop, hang you! You'll choke yourself to death with your laughing' (*ibid.*, 31).

Lucian stands in a long tradition of placing gods in a comical perspective. But while Homer's mockery was made within the frame of heroic deeds and epic narrative and bore witness to the immortality of the gods, and Aristophanes' burlesquing of the gods was made in a Saturnalian spirit of Dionysos' own feast, thereby revealing the transcendence of this god, Lucian parodied the old gods when and where he found a paying audience, exhibiting them as powerless and outdated. His laughter is critical. Lucian has been characterized as a *spoudogeloios*, a serious jester in the tradition of Socrates (Branham 1989: 26–8). This is, perhaps, to give him both too much and too little credit. For Socrates, humour was a vehicle for philosophy. Lucian, on the contrary, was an entertainer more than a philosopher. But like all good entertainment of the jesting variety, a good laugh is dependent on the exposure of hidden meanings with more serious implications. Lucian's mocking of the religious world of his time coincided with the pagan philosophical criticism, and for that matter, also with contemporary Christian criticism, as reflected for instance in Tertullian (*Apology*), Clement (*The Exhortation to the Greeks*) and Minucius Felix (*Octavius*). By ridiculing the cult of statues, the multiplicity of the gods, the gods in animal shapes, the oracles and the divine men, Lucian provided a striking image of religion in late antiquity as it was seen by educated and sceptical men.[6] Beneath Lucian's themes and the laughter they provoked lies the cultural tension which was the result of the cultural and religious changes in the Roman empire – a tension which was both sharpened and eased through critical laughter.

Lucian's procedure was to make abundant use of playful incongruities. He made fun of the gods by introducing traditional elements in a new context, by introducing the traditional gods to new situations and generally by making the gods uncomfortably like human beings. Lucian's anthropomorphic perspective is important. A recurrent theme in the criticism of the traditional gods was that they had become too human. One additional example is the Christian Minucius Felix, who, to promote his own religion, made fun of the gods along similar lines as the pagan Lucian: 'If gods are born, why pray are no gods born to-day? Can it be perhaps that Jupiter has become aged, and Juno past child-bearing, and Minerva grey before becoming a mother?' (*Octavius*, 21, 11).

We might, however, turn this accusation of anthropomorphism around, and ask if the real problem was rather that it was impossible for the traditional gods to become human enough. The flourishing of the mystery cults with gods who knew human pain and passion, and the later victory of Christianity with a god who had become flesh and blood on earth, indicate that part of the reason why the traditional gods were repeatedly the focus of laughter was that they remained isolated in their divine world.

So while critical laughter is a human laughter aimed at the gods of ancient tradition, it is also witness to a new way of looking at human beings and their place in the world. It is a self-conscious laughter appearing at that time in history when the human form is on the verge of becoming a central symbolic medium.

ANIMALS AND MYSTERIES

The mystery gods clearly 'humanized' religion. But the new cults and foreign gods did not in any way escape the laughter that had mocked the traditional gods. For instance, Lucian said of the mystery gods:

> Whereas many outsiders, not only Greek but foreigners as well, quite unworthy of sharing our citizen privileges, fraudu-lently enrolled somehow and passing off as gods, have filled the heavens, so that our feasting chamber is crowded with a disorderly mob of fellows of many different languages and races, and whereas there is a shortage of ambrosia and nectar, so that a half pint now costs a fortune owing to the great number of drinkers, and whereas they have wilfully thrust aside the real gods and claimed the front seats for themselves,

contrary to all the traditions of our forefathers and want to
have preferential honour on earth . . .

(*The Assembly of the Gods*, 14–15, in MacLeod 1991: 65)

In this passage, Lucian labelled both older gods from abroad and the
new mystery gods as 'foreigners'. He was far from alone in his mocking view. Several of the authors of his day aimed their barbs at the
oriental cults, especially those coming from Egypt. Egyptian religion
was the subject of Roman ridicule for several reasons. Egypt was
perceived as an old high culture with an exotic religion; moreover,
there was longstanding political tension between Rome and Egypt.
Prominent Romans had flirted with the Egyptian cults, which were
spectacular and visible. The cult of the great Egyptian mother goddess Isis was popular, even among some of the emperors. Egyptian
religion was, to the Roman mind, the disturbing and exciting Other.

Many educated Romans, however, turned up their noses at the
Egyptian cults; they delighted in scoffing at the urban Isis and her
cult with its myth about the murder of her husband, Osiris, and the
goddess' sorrow. Osiris was twice murdered, for after his death, his
corpse was stolen and dismembered. Isis goes out in search of it.
Her joy is great when she eventually regains the corpse and manages to
have Osiris buried. Osiris rises again in the Underworld and becomes
its king; their son, Horus, rules the earth. The emotions of the gods
were acted out in the cult: people wept, wailed, and wounded themselves when Osiris died, and shouted with joy when he was found.

When the Egyptian Isis was ridiculed, the spectacular sorrow and
subsequent joy of her adherents were particularly scorned by outsiders. This joy is, of course, an example of regenerative laughter,
now become an object of scorn. The fact that the worshippers of
Isis and Osiris underwent the same cycle of emotions each year is
found ridiculous; Ovid pokes fun at Osiris, who according to him
is never sufficiently sought after (*Metamorphoses*, 9, 693, cf. Heyob
1975: 55). Juvenal ridicules the joy and shouting that followed when
Osiris was found (*Satire*, VIII, 29). Augustine refers with delight to
the philosopher Seneca who amused himself at the great moaning
when Osiris was lost and the joy when he was found, though the
people who grieved and rejoiced in reality had neither lost nor
gained anything at all (*De Civitate Dei*, 6, 10). A similar point is made
by Minucius Felix: 'Isis rejoices, her priests jump for joy, the *Cynocephalus* glories in his discovery; and year by year, they cease not to
lose what they find or to find what they lose' (*Octavius*, 23, 1).

The *Cynocephalus*, 'doghead', is a mocking designation of Anubis, a central god in the mystery cult of Isis and Osiris. Anubis was the companion of the dead souls, and featured wholly or partly in animal shape. Anubis and his like were frequently targets of Roman jokes. The most ridiculed aspect of Egyptian religion was the strong tendency of its gods to show themselves in animal forms, both in mythological conceptions and statues, and *in vivo* in the Apis bull of Osiris and the Mnevis bull of Ptah. The Romans felt contempt for these animals and hybrids (Smelik and Hemelrijk 1984). Juvenal suspected that their worshippers did not take them seriously either. When the people mourned Osiris, Juvenal says, a priest with the mask of a dog personifying Anubis laughed at the mourners: 'Hence the chief and highest place of honour is awarded to Anubis, who, with his linen-clad and bald crew, mocks at the weeping of the people as he runs along' (*Satire*, VI, 532–4).

Lucian found that the animal gods from Egypt exceeded all reason. As he puts it in his well-known style:

> However, gods, all these things I've mentioned are within bounds, but, you dog-faced Egyptian swathed in linens, who are *you*, my excellent fellow? How do *you* claim to be a god, *you* with your barking? And what's the meaning of this spotted bull from Memphis being worshipped, giving oracles and having prophets? For I'm ashamed to mention the ibises, apes, goats and other creatures much more ludicrous, which have somehow been stuffed into heaven from Egypt. How, gods, can you bear to see them being worshipped equally or even more than yourselves? Or how can *you* endure it, Zeus, when they make you grow a ram's horns?
>
> (*The Assembly of the Gods*, 10, in MacLeod 1991: 61–3)

Egyptian animal worship was somewhat of a standing joke in late antiquity. Contemporaries of the Egyptians obviously found such cults funny. Like other authors of his time, Clement of Alexandria mocked Egyptian temples and their cults of animals. In one passage, Clement takes us to meet a priest who sings a solemn hymn and then pulls back the curtain a little to show the Egyptian god. Then we shall laugh about the object of worship, says Clement:

> There is no god within, whom we were so anxiously looking for; there is only a cat, or a crocodile, or a snake native to the land, or some other similar animal suited for life in a cave or

den or in the mud, but certainly not in a temple. The god of the Egyptians, then, turns out to be only a beast curled up on a rich purple pillow.

(Paidagogos, 3, 4)

However, the denigration of animal worship is not restricted to the Egyptian cults. Clement, for instance, exclaims to the Greeks: 'you who never let a day pass without laughing at the Egyptians' (for their animal worship), and then goes on to accuse the Greeks of animal worship as well (*The Exhortation to the Greeks*, II, 34. cf. also Tertullian, *Apology*, 16, 13; Cicero, *De Natura Deorum*, 1, 36, 10). Even Clement's own religion was not exempt from the accusation of flirting with the animal form. Tertullian mentions a particular mockery from his own city of Carthage:

But quite recently in this city a new representation of our god has been displayed, since a certain person, a criminal hired to dodge wild beasts in the arena, exhibited a picture with this inscription: 'The God of the Christians, ass-begotten.' It had ass's ears; one foot was a hoof; it carried a book and wore a toga.

(Apology, 16, 12)

Tertullian strikes back, 'We laughed at both the name and the shape' *(ibid.,*16, 13), and continues by accusing the pagans of animal worship. This type of caricature was not restricted to Carthage. A similar type was found in 1856 in Rome, on the Palatine, in the form of a graffito. It had been sketched on the wall of the Pedagogium and reveals a crucified man with the head of an ass. At the foot of the cross is another man. The sketch is accompanied by the following text: 'Alexamenos worships his god.' Such representations may be connected with a pagan mockery related to the Jews; it was said that the Jews worshipped an ass, a man with the head of an ass, or simply the head of an ass, in the Holy of Holies in the temple of Jerusalem. Accordingly, Christ, the son of this god, could also be caricatured in the form of an ass.

These examples demonstrate that certain themes – such as the ridiculousness of animal worship – recurred when rhetoricians and others sought to laugh at religions. This recurrence may depend on a certain universality in what is ridiculed (animals posing as humans or gods are so easily conceived of as funny), but it is also a witness to certain changes in the ancient world-view. Animal worship had symbolized a connection to the natural world which Romans disclaimed, as did many of their neighbours. The mockery of the divine in animal form reflects the fact that the connection between human beings and the cosmos had begun to shift. Creatures of the animal world were no longer found worthy of religious roles in their own right. Animals were creatures to be tamed or beaten; they were to serve merely practical functions, such as providing food and fun. (The Roman games with their mass slaughters continued long after Christianity became victorious.)

The Egyptians, Mesopotamians and Greeks had upheld a view of the sacred cosmos in which human beings had a relationship with gods above and animals below (Detienne 1979). The Christian religion created a discourse focused on human beings and the relationship between God, soul and body. As the religious focus shifted from the natural world to human beings and their spiritual life, the animal form was no longer a medium through which one could reach God, and animals were laughed out of heaven.

THE DIVINE MAN AND THE MOCKING OF CHRISTIANITY

As higher truths were to an increasing degree expressed through the human form, the divine man who could provide connections with the divine became popular (Anderson 1994, Bieler 1935–6, Wilken 1984). At the same time, he became, of course, a target for malicious laughter. Some holy men claimed to be gods or sons of gods, others came to announce a new deity. They were known as miracle workers, magicians, astrologers or soothsayers, and were easily criticized for their idealized views of the world. Again we turn to Lucian. In his *Alexander*, Lucian gives a spiteful caricature of a divine man in late antiquity when he scorns the cult of Alexander of Abonoteichos. Lucian saw Alexander as a criminal and a swindler:

> To sum up, picture to yourself a mixture of deceit, cunning, and general wickedness, reckless audacity and executive ability, combined with a plausible manner that always made him seem better than he was, and completely contradicted his real intentions.
>
> (*Alexander*, 4, in Turner 1990: 222)

In the introduction to the text Alexander is praised for his divine appearance. But this appearance is fake; his hair is not all his own, he wears a toupee. His credibility is lost from the start because of that toupee. If his hair is false, what then about his 'miracles'? According to Lucian, Alexander established his divinity by first burying a brass plate in a temple of Apollo, thus proclaiming the arrival of Apollo and Asclepius in Abonoteichos. Alexander saw to it that the plate was discovered. Then he hid a small snake in a goose egg in the foundations of a new temple. He himself dug out the plastered egg in front of a vast audience, cracked it and revealed the snake and claimed it was Asclepius. Afterwards, he made a spectacular show of sitting in a semi-dark room with the serpent Glycon. He had a big, tame snake coiled around him, pretending that it was the one that had been found. The real head of the snake was hidden in Alexander's cloak and a false head – a cross between a man and a dog – spoke through a clever system of pipes operated by his helpers. By means of this artificial animal, Alexander faked oracles by receiving sealed questions, developing various methods of removing the seals, writing answers and then making the seals seem as if they never had been broken. The cult of Glycon flourished; 'icons, images, and bronze or silver statuettes of the new god were on sale everywhere' (*Alexander*, 18, in Turner 1990: 229). Alexander took high fees for his oracles and 'had a large number of employees – attendants, detectives, script-writers, librarians, copying-clerks, seal-experts, and interpreters – who had to be paid appropriate salaries' (*Alexander*, 23, in Turner 1990: 231–2). Lucian gives us a glimpse into the business side of Alexander's religious activity. In *Alexander*, a new religious system is thoroughly exposed as a swindle and subjected to laughter. Alexander was evidently not the divine man who would bring religion down to earth.

Lucian treated the Sophist Peregrinus, who had been a Christian, similarly to Alexander. Peregrinus' main fame rested on his spectacular death: after the Olympic games in 165 AD, he threw himself on a pyre. Lucian's picture of Peregrinus is unkind, to say the least. He describes him as an exhibitionist. When he gives his opinion of the Sophist's planned death to a weeping audience, Lucian's Epicurean mouthpiece makes a great show of how Peregrinus laughed himself to pieces (*On the Death of Peregrinus*).

Lucian obviously did not reflect general opinion when he derided contemporary religious heroes. Alexander was commemorated on coins, and Peregrinus seems to have been held in generally high esteem by his contemporaries. Yet, in *Alexander* and *On the Death of Peregrinus*, Lucian's laughter successfully tears off the masks of these religious heroes. While adherents viewed Alexander and Peregrinus in connection with holy lore and old mythology, Lucian describes them in the context of mundane life and worldly gain. In the opposition between the perspectives of adherents and of Lucian, incongruities could be revealed and critical laughter could be used.

When Lucian wrote about Peregrinus, Christianity was not yet widespread.[7] He made fun of Christians, but they were not his main target. Yet even if Lucian's sarcasm about the Christians is mild, his descriptions of the peculiarities of the new Christian cult are typical. They reflect the views of an educated outsider who had never been a Christian, never studied their beliefs and probably never read their texts (Betz 1959). He satirizes their belief in immortality, their willingness to die, their brotherly love for each other, their denial of the Greek gods and their worship of 'that crucified sophist'. He patronizes their great gullibility and sees them in general as fools (*On the Death of Peregrinus*, 13, in MacLeod 1991: 155).

An easy way to ridicule Christians and to create comical incongruities was to contrast reality and appearance, to take literally what was meant to be taken symbolically. One example is the pagan Celsus, who found the idea of the resurrection of the body and the veneration of the cross laughable, and who ridiculed these beliefs in an ironical passage. The Christian exegete and theologian Origen, who handed down Celsus' criticism, did not find it funny at all (cf. Wilken 1984: 96):

> And everywhere they speak in their writings of the tree of life and of resurrection of the flesh by the tree – I imagine because their master was nailed to a cross and was a carpenter by trade. So that if he had happened to be thrown off a cliff, or pushed into a pit, or suffocated by strangling, or if he had been a cobbler or stonemason or blacksmith, there would have been a cliff of life above the heavens, or a pit of resurrection, or a rope of immortality, or a blessed stone, or an iron of love, or a holy hide of leather. Would not an old woman who sings a story to lull a little child to sleep have been ashamed to whisper tales such as these?
>
> (*Contra Celsum*, 6, 34)

However, we learn more about anti-Christian jests from the Christians themselves than from their adversaries. Several of the Christian apologists refer to the mockeries of their contemporaries. From Tertullian, we learn that non-Christians must have laughed at the prospect of Christ's resurrection from the dead: 'Laugh at what you will,' says Tertullian, 'but let them [the demons] laugh with you!' (*Apology*, 23, 13). In his usual style, he promises the mockers eternal damnation. Yet, Tertullian admits that he too had found Christian beliefs laughable before he became a Christian: 'Yes! we too in our day laughed at this', and with his famous sentence: 'We are from among yourselves. Christians are made, not born!' (*Apology*, 18, 4), he points to the common cultural background which both Christians and pagans shared.

FAREWELL TO LAUGHTER

The critical laughter of the second and third centuries reflected an upper-class uneasiness with old traditions and popular religion as well as with new and foreign cults. It was a laughter of outsiders, a rhetorical device in which reason opposed emotions. This controlled laughter was directed at outdated conceptions of the gods. It parodied the superficial and spectacular features of religions which were accessible to everyone. The beliefs and ideas that were singled out for mockery tell us much about common cultural concerns and tensions. Some of these tensions are linked to changes in the conception of the relationship between human beings and the world. Critical laughter was instrumental in stripping the natural world and its inhabitants of their sacredness and preparing the ground for the human form to be made divine. In the words of Clement: 'Do not believe that stones and stocks and birds and snakes are sacred things, while men are not. For rather regard men as really sacred, and take beasts and stones for what they are' (*The Exhortation to the Greeks*, 10). Thus, critical laughter was an integral part of an historical process in which old religions were swept away as a new religion emerged.

It is not surprising that with the ascendance of Christianity, the traditional sources of laughter were attacked, and the laughter culture of the Roman world was gradually forced into retreat. Christianity was a religion of words and texts. In Christianity God is modelled on language, not on forces of nature. When religious symbolism centres around literal texts and on an ideal human body, marked by chastity and a continent life, laughter is bound to become a stranger.

Most of the official entertainment in the Roman empire had been intertwined with pagan religions. Tertullian wrote a venomous treatise, *On the Spectacular*, which is notable for its reflection of an unvarnished Christian opinion about such entertainment. Tertullian compared the worldly joys of the pagans with the future happiness of the Christians, 'things of greater joy than circus, theatre or amphitheatre, or any stadium' (*De Spectaculis*, 30). He reserves his laughter not for the comedies of his day, but for the great show at the end of the world, where all the entertainers will be roasted in the eternal fire:

> And then there will be the tragic actors to be heard, more vocal in their own tragedy; and the players to be seen, lither of limb by far in the fire; and then the charioteers to watch, red all over in the wheel of flame; and next, the athletes to be gazed upon, not in their gymnasiums but hurled in the fire – unless it be that not even then would I wish to see them, in my desire rather to turn an insatiable gaze on them who vented their rage and fury on the Lord.
>
> (*De Spectaculis*, 30)

So much for entertainment!

Not only theatres, but also classic texts were attacked. In one of Clement's ironical outbursts, he comments on a beloved passage in Homer, the Ares/Aphrodite episode.[8] Clement says bluntly: 'Cease the song, Homer. There is no beauty in that; it teaches adultery. We have declined to lend even our ears to fornication' (*The Exhortation to the Greeks*, 4, 52). The passage Clement comments upon had been a source of erotic laughter for several hundred years. When Clement rejects it, his statement points forward to later Christian conceptions of laughter, in which laughter was systematically seen in connection with the lustful body, and condemned.

59

4

EARLY CHRISTIANITY
Laughter between body and spirit

In the previous chapter, we moved in the great world of the Roman empire. We have glimpsed a variety of religions, listened to writers who mocked the traditional gods and ridiculed each others' beliefs, and caught echoes of the laughing audience. In this chapter, we remain in the Roman empire, but our focus now turns to the complexity of early Christianity. In Christianity from the first to the fourth century, we meet the first attempts to create a theology of laughter. We encounter the question of whether the historical Jesus ever laughed, and find monks and virgins urged to keep a serious face. We will also become acquainted with the laughing saviour of the challengers to mainstream Christianity, the Gnostics, and the role laughter played within their texts. Above all, we find that in Christianity laughter becomes a spiritual phenomenon.

The first time we find laughter in a Christian text is in the New Testament, the Sermon on the Plain in the gospel of Luke:[1] 'Blessed are you who weep now; for you will laugh'; 'Woe to you who are laughing now! for you will mourn and weep' (Luke 6: 21, 6: 25)[2] These sayings are stamped with a negative attitude towards gaiety in this life, combined with an expectation of great happiness to come, at least for some. The contrast made between laughter and weeping is not new. We have seen it, for instance, in Demeter's story. What is new is that this contrast is no longer part of an opposition between two phases in a ritual or two seasons of the year as in earlier times. It has become a contrast between this world and the next. What is at stake is no longer the seasonal renewal of life, but the salvation of human beings. Laughter has moved out of the present world and has become a subject of eschatology and apocalypticism, a sign of the joy which will be released at the end of time. The critique of wordly laughter reflected in the sayings from Luke found fruitful ground in the early Church and took root.

Laughter had also been a theme in the Near Eastern wisdom tradition. Even if there are exceptions, laughter has seldom fared well in any wisdom tradition, whose adherents may have been too focused on cultivating rationality to appreciate such a boisterous human expression as laughing. Christian theologians quoted with delight the words of the pessimistic Ecclesiastes, about laughter being foolish and the fool's laughter being as crackling thorns under a pot (2: 2, 3: 1–8, 7: 6)[3]

CHURCH FATHERS AND DESERT FATHERS

While the Greek philosophers laid the cornerstone of a laughter theory, the Christian Church Fathers made laughter a subject of theology. As we saw in chapter 3, one of the first Christian thinkers who bothered himself with the subject was Clement of Alexandria. In *Paidagogos*, he devoted a special discussion to laughter. Clement demanded that even smiling must be kept under control and made the subject of discipline. Because sudden laughter wreaks violence on rational discourse, it must be regulated, even if it is natural to human beings:

> We need not take away from man any of the things that are natural to him, but only set a limit and due proportion to them. It is true that man is an animal who can laugh; but it is not true that he therefore should laugh at everything. The horse is an animal that neighs, yet he does not neigh at everything.

> (*Paidagogos*, 2, 46)

Clement's ambition was not to quench laughter completely, but to regulate it. It should be kept in check and used moderately. Why does Clement concern himself with laughter? Because laughter was associated with the body, which Clement and other Church Fathers believed must be controlled. Clement's uneasiness about laughter is in accordance with the Stoic ideal of late antiquity, that is, that reason ought to conquer emotions. As we have seen earlier, an obvious consequence of the celebration of reason is that laughter becomes a disturbing element (chapter 3). In its inarticulate outbursts, laughter violates rational thought and speech. Clement dictated that discourse should be controlled, the voice gentle and the words clearly articulated, reflecting a soul that was filled with the words of God (Brown 1989: 122–39). Clement even gave advice on table- and bed-manners. His ideal of composure, self-command and restraint is evident everywhere. In short, excessive laughter reveals weakness of character and destroys discipline. Only a moderate laughter fit Clement's ideal of a well-behaved Christian.

Clement shared this elite view of laughter not only with Greek and Roman philosophers, but also with leaders from other religions, Egyptians as well as Jews. According to Chaeremon, the teacher of the emperor Nero, the Egyptian priests seldom laughed, and if they felt the urge, they only smiled, because laughter was incompatible with their priestly dignity (van der Horst 1987). Laughing was also unsuitable for the Jewish rabbis, and the student of Torah should only allow himself a 'minimum of laughter' (*Avot*, VI, 5, in Reines 1972: 182).

However, the peak of Christian aversion toward laughter was not reached with Clement. Over the next centuries it became clear that there was more to this aversion than late antiquity's considerations about decorum and discipline, as typical Christian discourse on laughter gradually developed. Whether in the East or the West, the learned men of the early Church – such as Ambrose, Jerome, Basil, Pseudo-Cyprian and John Chrysostom – are unanimous in their hostility toward laughter (Adkin 1985, Resnick 1987). The more it was the focus of hostility, however, the more symbolic significance accrued to laughter. Laughter attained a new religious significance, not as a genuine religious expression, but as a symbol of that which must be shunned by those whose power derived from their religious virtuosity. Paradoxically, laughter acquired symbolic value from its absence rather than from its presence.

John Chrysostom, Bishop of Constantinople, is known as the first to point out that Jesus never laughed (Resnick 1987: 96–7). Instead he stressed that Jesus wept twice, once when he beheld Jerusalem, and the second time when Lazarus was raised from the dead. John Chrysostom found mourning most suitable on earth, considering the state of the present world. In connection with the life and suffering of Christ he repeatedly and rhetorically asks his audience 'dost thou laugh?' (*Homilies on Hebrews*, XV). To be fair, John Chrysostom, like Clement earlier, did not want to do away with *all* laughter. He aimed his criticism at the excess of laughter, laughter beyond measure and out of control. All the same, his homilies give the impression that there is something profoundly suspicious about laughter. To give vent to amusement was often the first step on the road to perdition. The steps between laughter and grievous sin could be few:

> For example; to laugh, to speak jocosely, does not seem an acknowledged sin, but it leads to acknowledged sin. Thus laughter often gives birth to foul discourse, and foul discourse to actions still more foul. Often from words and laughter proceed railing and insult; and from railing and insult, blows and wounds; and from blows and wounds slaughter and murder.
>
> *(Concerning the Statues, Homily, XV)*

When John Chrysostom contrasts those who are now laughing with their grinding and gnashing of teeth on the last day, an imagery of grinning skulls and death as a laughing monster seeps through the text. (We also recall Tertullian's making fun of actors, whom Tertullian foresaw as burning in eternal fire).

> When therefore thou seest persons laughing, reflect that those teeth, that grin now, will one day have to sustain that most dreadful wailing and gnashing, and that they will remember this same laugh on That Day whilst they are grinding and gnashing! Then thou too shalt remember this laugh!
>
> *(Concerning the Statues, Homily, XX)*

John Chrysostom's criticism of laughter is more thoroughgoing than Clement's. In Chrysostom's time, at the end of the fourth century AD, two hundred years after Clement, there seems to have been a shared opinion among leaders of the Church that laughter challenged virtue and led to laxity. But the aversion against laughter was no longer primarily a question of reason and manners as had been the case with Clement, when it reflected a general opinion among educated men at his time. Rather, laughter was now conceived of as undermining the very foundations of the ascetic life from which the Christian Church was nourished. As John Chrysostom stressed, the thought of the suffering and death of Jesus on the cross ought to quench all laughter, once and for all. Within Christianity there were some who battled especially hard against worldly laughter – the Christian hermits and monks.

Monks and hermits were, more than anyone else, expected to renounce the world so as to inscribe religion on their very bodies. Separated from their fellow beings, under great hardship, the hermits and monks in Egypt, Syria and Palestine renounced the world, kept themselves chaste, were clothed in rags, seldom washed, slept little, did not eat meat or drink wine and lived in caves, or settled on the top of pillars. They were highly respected; their extreme holiness made a deep impression. When laughter is mentioned in connection with them, it is with negativity: 'Swearing, making false oaths, lying, getting angry, insulting people, laughing, all that is alien to monks' (*Apophthegmata Patrum*, in Ward 1981: 155). Weeping, on the contrary, was meritorious, and the monks had much to cry over: the crucifixion of Jesus; constant awareness of their sins; fear for the demons who continually tempted and tormented the monks; terror of eternal damnation. In short, the monks cried over the miseries of this world. According to legend, Arsenios cried so hard that his eyelids fell off. Of another Desert Father, Abba John, nicknamed 'the Dwarf', it is said that when he saw one of the brothers laugh at the agape, the meal they ate after Mass, he started to cry: 'What does this brother have in heart, that he should laugh, when he ought to weep, because he is eating at an *agape*' (*Apophthegmata Patrum*, in Ward 1981: 339). In Abba John's opinion, the monks should rather have concentrated upon the suffering and death of Jesus.

The firm stand of ascetic Christianity against laughter was not without precedent. The Pythagoreans boasted that Pythagoras never laughed (Bremmer 1992). For the Essenes, a Jewish group living at the Dead Sea, laughter was reason for punishment: 'Whoever has guffawed foolishly shall do penance for thirty days' (*The Community Rule*, in Vermes 1990: 71).[4] In other words, the Christians shared with Greek and Jewish ascetics the ideal of the perfect human who never laughed (Adkin 1985; Resnick, 1987). The classical model is evident in Athanasius' description of Saint Anthony. Anthony was one of the first who went into the desert in Egypt. Like the saints Eugendus and Martin of Tours he was famous for never having laughed (Bartelink 1994: 173–5).[5] But why was it so necessary for the Christian monks and hermits to renounce laughter? One might propose, for instance, that since these men led an evangelical life, the good news of the gospel might be reflected in their merry countenance and joyful attitude. But laughter was clearly regarded as suspicious.

Nor were these saints unique among the Christians. The oldest monastic rule – Pachom's from Egypt (fourth century) – forbade the Pachomian monks to joke, and they were punished if they laughed at prayer and meal-times (*Precepts*, 8 and 31; Adkin 1985: 151–2). Ammonius, the disciple of Anthony, insisted that the monks ought never to laugh. In a speech against laughter, the Syrian Ephraem paints the dangers of laughter vividly:

Laughter is the beginning of destruction of soul; o monk, when you notice something of that, know that you have arrived at the depth of the evil. Then do not cease to pray God, that he might rescue you from this death ... Laughter expels the virtues and pushes aside the thoughts on death and meditation on the punishment.

(Frank 1964: 145)

The Cappadocian father, Basil, maintained that the Christian 'ought not to indulge in jesting; he ought not to laugh nor even to suffer laughmakers' (*On the Perfection of the Life of Solitaries, Letter*, 22). Basil prescribed that whoever laughed in the monastery was to be expelled for one week (*Epitemia*, 7, in Adkin 1985: 152). In Italy, *The Rule of the Master* from the sixth century mentions laughter as one of those vices which ought not to occur in monastic life. From roughly the same time, *The Rule of St. Benedict*, on which life in Western monasteries is based, urged the monks: 'Prefer moderation in speech and speak no foolish chatter, nothing just to provoke laughter; do not love immoderate or boisterous laughter' (4, 52–4). It absolutely condemned 'in all places any vulgarity and gossip and talk leading to laughter' (6, 8 and 49, 7). This *Rule* includes Benedict's famous ladder to humility. Of the ladder's twelve steps, the restraint against laughter constitutes the tenth step, while the eleventh is a warning against joking (7, 59–61). In Ireland, about one hundred years later, Columban's *Regula Coenobialis* transmits the same type of regulations against laughter as the older rules did, even if this rule gives us a glimpse of occasions when laughter at least may happen 'pardonably':

He who because of coughing in the beginning of the psalms does not sing out well is commanded to make amends by six strokes ... And he who smiles in the service ... six strokes; if he breaks out in the noise of laughter, a special fast unless it has happened pardonably.

(Resnick 1987: 95)

The many monastic rules against laughter demonstrate the power, albeit negative, that laughter was deemed to have. Laughter had to be conquered to control the body.

WEEPING VIRGINS

Similar to the hermetics and monks, another Christian group that was urged to exclude laughter from their lives were virgins. What did monks and virgins have in common that made it so important for them not to indulge in laughter?

'Let widows and virgins imitate her, let wedded wives make much of her, let sinful women fear her, and let bishops look up to her' (Jerome, *Letters*, 24, 5). These words of Jerome about Asella at the end of the fourth century reflect the Church's high regard for the virgin. The Church Fathers show a marked preoccupation with virginity; they preferred virgins to married women and saw them as the ideal type of Christian woman (Salisbury 1992). Among the things the virgins were to abstain from was laughing. Jerome, a brilliant letter-writer, wrote a famous letter on virginity addressed to Eustochium, who lived her virginal life as a nun and scholar in Bethlehem. In it, Jerome recommends that Eustochium should not laugh at jokes, which could encourage flatterers and was incompatible with a life devoted to God (*Letters*, 22, 24, l, Miller 1993). To another virgin, Demetrias, Jerome says, 'When you are present, buffoonery and loose talk must find no place' (*Letters*, 130, 13, 1), and he continues to praise two well-known Romans who had laughed only once in their lives. Jerome writes approvingly of Eustochium's mother, the late Paula, who wanted to make up for all her laughing by constant weeping: 'Her tears welled forth as it were from fountains, and she lamented her slightest faults as if they were sins of the deepest dye' (*Letters*, 108, 15, 1).

Other Fathers were just as critical of laughing virgins as Jerome was (Adkin 1985). Ambrose argued that when laughter creeps in modesty is relaxed (*Concerning Virgins*, 3, 3, 9); John Chrysostom maintained that a virgin must avoid not only a striking display of joy, but even the slightest smile. In an address especially to women, John Chrysostom mentions laughter in the same breath as carnal desire. Like Jerome, Ambrose and their colleagues, Chrysostom saw a close connection between laughter and lack of chastity (Adkin 1985). Obviously laughter was perceived as a thin veil over carnality – sexual impulses lurked behind it. The Fathers did not want any of those sexual impulses aroused, for they were the greatest danger to the virginal life.

The Christian opposition to laughter is prominent in the context of the ideal of the virginal life. Christians shared their dislike of laughter with Egyptian priests, Jewish rabbis and Pythagorean ascetics; like them, they were concerned about dignity and reason. But the Christians were motivated by more than a concern about demeanour: the human body from which laughter emanated had gained a profound symbolic significance in Christianity. In monastic and virginal life, this bodily symbolism was at its most extreme.

The ascetic life of monks and virgins was characterized by sexual renunciation; the body was closed to the world. In accordance with this ideal, virgins were pale and thin; they fasted, prayed and kept within doors. Outside, they were veiled to avoid men's gaze. Eustochium is compared to the ark that contained nothing but the tablets of the covenant; she was to give no thought to anything that was outside.[6] These admonitions reflect a discourse on the body that was typical for early Christianity. The more the body was closed against the world, the more the soul was opened up to God. The attitude of ascetic Christianity toward laughter must be evaluated in this context. Sexual activity, gluttony, drinking, feasting and laughter represent a maximum opening up toward life in this world. In particular, sexually active women represented vivid embodiments of this opening up. For all men, women were a temptation; for an ascetic, they were an even greater frustration. Jerome describes his temptations in the Syrian desert in intense language:

> Now, although in my fear of hell I had consigned myself to this prison, where I had no companions but scorpions and wild beasts, I often found myself amid bevies of girls. My face was pale and my frame chilled with fasting; yet my mind was burning with desire, and the fires of lust kept bubbling up before me when my flesh was as good as dead.
>
> (*Letters*, 22, 7)

The value of the virgin lay in her existence as a walking symbol of the closed body, a negation of the phantom temptresses of Jerome, an ideal to be cherished and held in awe (Miller 1994). In the words of the bridal imagery from the Song of Songs, the virginal body was 'a closed door' 'a closed garden', or 'a fountain' which was sealed (Salisbury 1992: 29–30). Anything that threatened this closure was evil; thus laughter, an expression of a symbol of a body being opened up toward the world, was forbidden.

Within early Christianity, a more profound criticism of laughter than we saw in Greco-Roman philosophy developed. For Christians, laughter was a deeply serious matter. Why did the Church take laughter so seriously? One answer is that Christian life was consistently seen in the larger symbolic context of the battle with the body (Stroumsa 1990). Laughter revealed that the body was still open toward the world and that control over it was incomplete. So while humans by nature may be the only creatures capable of laughter – in Clement's words, a human being was 'a rational, mortal, terrestrial, walking, laughing animal' (*Stromateis*, VIII, 6) – the goal was not to cultivate natural man. On the contrary, the goal of human beings must be to transcend their nature and be spiritualized (Resnick 1987: 98–9). Laughter was regarded as a crack through which earthly matters could touch the human soul. When the body was regarded as a vehicle for salvation, that sort of crack was no small matter.

DID ANYONE LAUGH?

Despite the Church Fathers' best efforts, laughter was never completely shut out of Christian life. We know, for instance, of John Chrysostom's complaint that his congregation burst out laughing when it should have prayed (*Homilies on the Epistle to the Hebrews*, XV, 8). Furthermore, the monastic rules against laughter found everywhere in the Christian world indirectly reveal that there still must have been much merriment among the monks; in some cases, laughter might even 'happen pardonably'. If no one had laughed, there would have been no need for rules against it. Laughing Christians were found within the monk cells and monasteries; jokes even entered the *vitae sanctorum*, the descriptions of the lives of the saints.

In *The Sayings of the Desert Fathers*, we read that no one ever saw a smile on Father Pambo's face. He behaved in other words as a real saint. The demons noticed this, and they decided to try to trick him into laughing. They put wing feathers on a lump of wood and brought it in while they cried, 'Go, go'. When Father Pambo saw them, he started to laugh. The demons exclaim, 'Ha, Ha, Pambo has laughed'. But he answered them, 'I have not laughed, but I made fun of your powerlessness, because it takes so many of you to carry a wing' (*Apophthegmata Patrum*, in Ward 1981: 197). In this way Pambo fooled the demons. His pious laughter at evil was not only allowed, but transformed into an heroic deed.

This ambiguous attitude to laughter can be traced further in several texts. In these texts the suppression of laughter is combined with the promotion of a joking attitude. For instance, according to tradition, Lawrence, a deacon who suffered martyrdom on a red-hot grill in Rome, cracked a gruesome joke to his tormentors, 'Turn me around, I am really roasted on that side' (Curtius 1953: 425–6). Even if the saints Anthony and Martin did not laugh, it was said that Anthony's speech was spiced with 'divine wit' and that Martin joked in a pious way.[7] And in one of his letters, Athanasius says that a virgin's laughter must be soft and radiant with divine beauty (Adkin 1985: 151, n. 5). What can we make of this last admonition – an apparent contradiction to the rules against virgins laughing at all?

The key to what was regarded as acceptable laughter and joking among Christian monks and virgins seems to be the word 'pious': pious laughter expressed spiritual joy, never carnal desires. Salvation worked by means of the body, and the body could, in accordance with the thinking of Jerome, either develop into a temple for the Holy Spirit or into a brothel. Likewise, laughter could be a sign either of spiritual awareness or of spiritual ruin. The laughter the ideal Christian was repeatedly warned against was the laughter of carnality. Another aspect of Christian laughter was the laughter of spirituality. Spiritual joy could be reflected in a smile. Of Martin, the leader of a community of ascetics and later Bishop of Tours, it was said that no one had ever seen him angry, agitated, sad or laughing, but that his face was radiant with heavenly joy (Sulpicius Severus, *Vita Sancti Martini*, 27). Spiritual laughter was not related to the body; it was seen as a reflection of a Christian soul.

THE LUDICROUS JAHWEH AND THE LAUGHING CHRIST

One group of early Christians, however, embraced laughter and made explicit use of it in their texts. This group was regarded as the *enfants terribles* of the early Church – the Gnostics.

The Gnostics were important participants in the Christian movement, and they flourished at a time when Christian doctrine was not yet firmly established. Early Christianity was a complex phenomenon, and it was in part shaped through dialogue and conflict with Gnostic groups and their texts. But while the writings of the Church Fathers survived, the Gnostic texts were missing for over 1,500 years. Some of these texts were regained as early as in the nineteenth century. But in 1945, sensationally, a library was found at Nag Hammadi in Upper Egypt. It had been hidden since the fourth century, and contained thirteen books with fifty-three texts – many of them Gnostic (Robinson 1988).[8] These texts were found in the vicinity of a Pachomian monastery, suggesting that Gnostic texts were perhaps used as edifying literature for Christian monks.[9] It is likely that the Gnostic texts had been stored away when Bishop Athanasius of Alexandria issued a letter in AD 367 announcing which books Christians might read and which were to be avoided.

The texts reveal that the Gnostics had a dualistic outlook on the world. According to them, matter and spirit, body and soul, were fundamentally different from each other. In Gnostic thinking, the spiritual world was both present and hidden in the material world. The relationship between these two worlds was complex and difficult; the material world and its creations were perceived as imitations, reflections and shadows of the spiritual world and its manifestations. In this way the two worlds were related to each other and at the same time fundamentally different.

The Gnostics cultivated laughter in their writings, in which irony, paradox and comedy were frequently used. Gnostic laughter was largely a consequence of two things: first, Gnostic Christianity established itself in opposition to Jewish, pagan and Christian traditions and thus used the same sort of critical laughter as we have seen in the rhetoric of the second century. Second, in Gnosticism, the soul's salvation was dependent on *gnosis*, or knowledge. The process of acquiring salvific knowledge in Gnosticism was akin to solving a riddle or seeing the point of a joke. In opposition to the wisdom tradition, which had a more static conception of knowledge, the Gnostic approach was dynamic and incorporated the laughter of insight or understanding.

There were several Gnostic groups and movements. One Gnostic leader, Valentinus, who first taught in Egypt and was nearly elected Bishop in Rome in AD 140, later founded or inspired a separate Christian church whose doctrines had a philosophical orientation. In modern times, several Gnostic texts have been gathered under the name Sethian.[10] One of the outstanding characteristics of these texts is that Seth, the son of Adam and Eve, has a prominent place and a special significance. The Gnostic laughter myths are mainly found in this Sethian group of texts.[11]

The Gnostics' radical attacks on the Christian world did not stop short of taking Jahweh to task. Irony and mockery were used systematically to throw new light upon Biblical texts. 'Do not think it is, as Moses said', a smiling Jesus tells John in *Apocryphon of John* (CG, II, 1, 13: 17–21, 22: 9–15). The ironic perspective makes it clear that there are two types of understanding, the traditional and material understanding (linked with Moses), and the Gnostic and spiritual one (linked with Christ). In the *Second Treatise of the Great Seth*, the author plunges into a radical banter about the Old Testament and its heroes:

> For Adam was a laughingstock ... And Abraham and Isaac and Jacob were a laughingstock ... David was a laughingstock ... Solomon was a laughingstock ... The 12 prophets were laughingstocks ... Moses, a faithful servant, was a laughingstock ...
>
> (CG, VII, 2, 62: 27–64: 1, in Robinson 1988: 368)

The patriarchs and prophets were all laughingstocks because they did not know Christ. But the most ludicrous of them all was the creator of the world himself, Ialdabaoth, the Gnostic parody of Jahweh.[12] He was a material creature with a lion's head and a human body.[13] He thought he was the only god and said so. Because he thus revealed that he did not know anything about the spiritual world above him, the Gnostics held him in ridicule (CG, II, 5, 112: 25–9; also CG, VII, 2, 53: 27–54: 4, 64: 18–65: 1).

This myth about the ignorant creator is one of three Gnostic myths involving laughter. The others are a myth about Jahweh's rape of Eve and a myth about the crucifixion of Jesus (Gilhus 1991a). In all three cases laughter occurs as a reaction to a clash between a spiritual and a material comprehension of events. In Gnosticism, dualism functions as a matrix for incongruities and laughter.[14]

Because of the Gnostics' dualistic perspective, stressing the separation of spirit and matter, their writings often feature the same figure in both a spiritual and a material version. Thus, Eve was both a spiritual saviour and a material woman. Christ was a messenger from the world above while Jesus was a material being. The doubling of roles was confusing and often comic. The spiritual Eve and Christ roared with laughter because of the havoc they wreaked when the maker of this world did not recognize their material counterparts. Laughter was part of a new dualistic context where body and spirit were played out against each other and a bewildered Jahweh/Ialdabaoth was caught between them, appearing more like a buffoon than a lofty god.

The Gnostic narratives of the creation of human beings follow the myths of Genesis closely, but these narratives have a comical touch. In one important Gnostic text, the *Hypostasis of the Archons*,

Ialdabaoth and the archons, who are the 'rulers' of the material world, make Adam out of earth (Gilhus 1985). But they do not manage to blow life into him, even if they blow like storm winds; instead they appear as impotent and ludicrous (CG, II, 4, 88: 3–9). Adam receives life only when a spiritual woman, Eve, descends upon him. When Ialdabaoth and his helpers see the spiritual Eve, they go mad with lust and think that by mixing their seed in her, they will possess the spiritual element. But Eve fools them. She leaves her shadowy reflection and becomes a tree. The shadow of spirit is matter, consequently the rulers of the world are left with a material woman, while the spiritual woman transforms herself into the Tree of Life or the Tree of Knowledge. When Ialdabaoth and the archons rape what is left and thus get the material Eve pregnant, the spiritual Eve laughs at them because she has fooled them into raping a shadow (CG, II, 4, 89: 3–31. Cf. CG, II, 5, 115: 31-116: 33). This confusion of person and shadow is a universal comic theme with infinite possibilities for cultural variations. In this case it goes to the heart of Gnostic ideology: matter mistaken for spirit.[15]

The Gnostics also applied their double perspective to the story of the crucifixion. The Gnostics' interest in Jesus and his activity on earth was minimal.[16] Their Christ was a spiritual messenger and his knowledge was revealed after the crucifixion. In Gnosticism, the division between Jesus and Christ, like the split between the two Eves, was the cause of comic misunderstanding.

The comic misunderstanding connected to Christ is found, for instance, in the *Apocalypse of Peter*. The text opens with Christ sitting in the temple talking with Peter (CG, VII, 3, 81: 3–83: 15). When the priests and the people rush to kill them, Peter is afraid, but Christ tells him that the priests are blind. He bids Peter to cover his eyes so that he can understand their blindness. When Peter covers his eyes, he sees a vision of the priests and the people. He covers his ears to hear what they said. Christ repeats that the priests and the people are deaf and blind. Then Peter 'sees' the crucifixion. He sees Jesus being grasped by the priests and how they beat him on his hands and feet. Peter is confused because this happens at the same time as he sees another man on the cross, happy and laughing. Christ tells Peter that the one who laughs on the cross is the living Saviour. The one whom the priests hammer the nails into was the material Jesus.

Like the spiritual Eve, the spiritual Christ laughed at those who pursued the material Jesus, proving that they could not see the difference between spirit and matter.[17]

The Gnostics were strongly influenced by Judaism at the same time as they caricatured the Old Testament God. A comparison of laughter in Gnostic myths and God's laughter in the Old Testament shows that both types of laughter are mocking; as in the Old Testament, Gnostic laughter aims at the arrogant and the disbelieving. But the arrogant and disbelieving are not the same in Gnostic texts as they were in the Old Testament. The God of the Old Testament laughed at those who did not realize His almighty power. The Gnostics laughed at those who mistook matter for spirit; their mockery emerged out of their dualistic outlook. The laughter of the Gnostics is diametrically opposed to the laughter in the Old Testament. In the Old Testament, God laughed at humans. In the Gnostic myths, human beings laugh at Jahweh. Jahweh had lost his power.

Humour thrives on the incongruous, in which an act or event is interpreted in two different perspectives at the same time. At first a predictable traditional perspective prevails. Then suddenly another perspective is introduced. The second perspective is unexpected and untraditional, and the clash between the two creates comedy. Comedy is especially effective when power is its subject, and the ludicrous effect is strengthened when that power does not understand that it is fooled, as was the case with Jahweh/Ialdabaoth. The Gnostics knew the traditional perspective of the biblical texts in which Jahweh was the indisputable God. The Gnostic texts presuppose that their audience had a basic knowledge of Christianity and the Old Testament. The comical effect of the myths of the rape of Eve and the crucifixion of Jesus were dependent on the Gnostic versions being mentally held up against their orthodox counterparts. Their effect would have been enlarged if the audience not only knew of but had also once believed in the traditional Jahweh.

GNOSTIC MYTHOLOGY

In the myths about the rape of Eve and the crucifixion of Jesus the Gnostics mocked the creation myths of the Old Testament as well as a core Christian belief. Both Gnostic myths share a common structure, a common theme and a common function. If we look closely at the structure of the myths, we can find these common elements:

1 spiritual being descends into the material world;
2 the cosmic powers wish to conquer (rape/kill) the spiritual being;

3   spiritual being mocks the cosmic powers and laughs at them;
4   spiritual being escapes;
5   the cosmic powers conquer the material shadow of the spiritual being;
6   the cosmic powers think they have conquered (raped/killed) the spiritual being.

The plight of Eve and the crucifixion of Jesus – myths which are different both in origin and semantics – are made to fit the same structural pattern. The laughter motif is one key to the understanding of how both these myths worked.

In Gnostic myth, laughter has a symbolic function which becomes evident in the Gnostic contrast between that which is opened up and that which is closed. We are reminded of the Christian Desert Fathers, monks and virgins and their anxiety about the body, which should remain closed to the world and thus opened up to God. The Gnostics exploited a similar contrast, but with a different purpose. The monks and virgins were to use their bodies to reach the spiritual. The Gnostic mythology, in contrast, eschewed the material, thereby seeking to liberate the spirit from its material prison. In spite of their dualistic perspective, though, Gnostic mythology is rich in bodily symbolism. For instance, while the acquiring of knowledge is a spiritual act, this act was often expressed using bodily metaphors.

Various adversaries of the Gnostics, mythological or real, are accused of blindness. They did not manage to see how things really were; they had no insight. Blindness is a form of closure against knowledge. Deafness is another. In the *Apocalypse of Peter*, the priests are accused of being both blind and deaf; they have understood nothing. On the other hand, when Peter covered his eyes and then his ears, he saw and heard what really happened. To be blind and deaf had, in other words, different meanings depending on the context. The key to understanding this difference is again the Gnostic dualistic conception of the world, with its sharp division between spirit and matter. Opening/closure can refer either to the material world or the spiritual world. To open oneself up to the material world meant to close oneself to the spiritual world and vice versa: when he closed himself to the material world, Peter understood what really happened on the spiritual level. His adversaries, on the contrary, were characterized as blind and deaf because they had closed themselves to the spiritual world.

The opponents of the Gnostics – closed to the spiritual world –

were portrayed as using bodily violence to force open the spiritual world. The archons opened Adam's side to get hold of the spiritual Eve. They tried to rape her. They nailed Jesus to the cross and crucified him. These violent openings of the body were aimed at grasping the spirit. But in vain: it is not possible to get hold of the spirit by means of physical violence. Gnosis is not mediated through forced openings. It is not bestowed through rape or crucifixion, but through spiritual awakening. In Gnosticism, laughter is a sign of receptivity; with it, the body literally speaking, opens up. As a symbol of choosing to open up, laughter is a contrast to the archons' attempts at opening the body by force, through rape and crucifixion.

Gnostic laughter is ambivalent; it encompasses both knowledge and mockery. It represents an opening up to salvific knowledge, as well as a mocking of those who reveal their lack of knowledge through their actions, typified in the world-creator Jahweh/Ialdabaoth. Plato taught that we laugh at those who embody the opposite of the advice from Delphi: know yourself. The Gnostics' goal was precisely to know who they were, from whence they came and where they were going. When their opponents were exposed, they were made ridiculous in Plato's meaning of the word, because they again and again revealed that they did *not* know themselves. As we have seen, the Gnostics were not alone in poking fun at the religious beliefs of their contemporaries. But they were different in that the group existed within the religion they mocked. They knew Christianity in detail, wanted to prove its insufficiency and short-comings, and thus achieve salvation. They did not, like Lucian, wish primarily to entertain, but rather to reform.

The Gnostics' laughter was closely connected with seeing through, understanding a point, acquiring new knowledge. The comic conveyed knowledge, an exploitation of the universal con-nection between wit and learning; 'ha-ha' and 'a-ha'. The frequent use of riddles, puns, paradoxes and jokes in Gnostic writings can be explained as techniques for keeping the spiritual and the material perspectives in tension, thus making them illuminate each other (Layton 1986). These comic techniques were vehicles to bring forth knowledge: *gnosis*. The resulting Gnostic myths are meant to work on their audience by means of their double references and gradually or abruptly make the audience open up to spiritual reality. The pur-pose of the myths was to hide and reveal simultaneously. Laughter represented a passage from the hidden to the revealed, it was malicious and full of knowledge, at the same time derisive and life-giving. This typically Gnostic laughter was a variant of the spiritual laughter of early Christianity, but with considerably more stress on the aspect of knowledge than on that of piety.

SPIRITUAL LAUGHTER

Even if the Gnostics had their laughter myths, which revealed a complex and sometimes sinister mentality, it is nowhere said that they were especially jolly. Rather, the function of laughter in the Gnostic texts was to make the audience understand. The laughter of the myths is a means to an end; the entertaining potential of the myths is exploited to reach a higher goal, namely to wake up sleeping souls to see their spiritual origin.

The Gnostics were participants in a larger general Christian discourse about the relationship between spirit and matter. They saw the body/soul relationship dualistically and made that relationship a major source of incongruity. With their two Eves, their Jesus opposed to Christ and their stupid world-creator, they played spirit and matter against each other and made a comic mythology out of their incompatibility. The laughter they cultivated in their mythology was sharp, and carved out its space between body and soul. In the process it cut apart thoughts and concepts which in mainstream Christianity constituted a sacred totality.

In mainstream Christianity, the body was supposed to be systematically worked upon to develop in a spiritual direction. But according to the Gnostics, only the spirit was important. The laughter of Gnostic mythology accentuated the difference between body and spirit and was instrumental in cutting the two apart. In the Christian text, the body was much more of an ambiguous phenomenon, and so, thus, was laughter.

Compared to the ideal laughter of monks and virgins, the laughter of Gnostic mythology has a certain aggressive edge to it. Even if we have legends like that of the pious Pambo, in which laughter is used as a weapon in the face of evil, as it also is in Gnostic texts, the Gnostic use of laughter has a systematically critical aspect which is generally not found in other Christian sources.

In spite of these differences, however, mainstream Christianity and Gnostic Christianity have in common a deep preoccupation with human beings and their spiritual life. Whether the access to this spiritual life is via the human body or via the soul, the preferred laughter is spiritual, mirroring either the piety of the soul or its *gnosis*. In both cases, spiritual laughter is a sign of a higher state of being, a human expression of the divine world.

Spiritual laughter is not the only type of laughter to be found in Christianity. Leaping forward in history to the twelfth century, we find that new types of bodily images have been generated, and laughter has once again become embodied.

5

MEDIEVAL CHRISTIANITY
Carnival, Corpus Christi and bodily laughter

In the high Middle Ages and the Renaissance, the body gained new significance. In the period from the twelfth to the sixteenth century new types of bodily images were generated. Truth became hidden in bodies, most prominently in the secrets of the suffering body of Christ, ripped open so that its interior truth shone forth. But the truth also hid in the flesh and bones of the saints. The broken and bleeding body of Christ was celebrated through art and through piety, and made accessible in the Mass. The Eucharist became the key symbol of Western Christianity, a religious approach in which 'a ritual which turned bread into flesh – a fragile, small wheaten disc into God' (Rubin 1991: 1) was central. Sermons, liturgy, prayers, hymns, theological expositions, drama and works of art from this period are testimonies to the revealed meanings of the Eucharist, but they are also pointers to the hidden and unspoken meanings of this ritual eating of divine flesh.

The approach to the body was not only through the figure of Christ or through the relics of the saints. Truth was also hidden in the young, male bodies of the Italian Renaissance. And it was hidden in the grotesque body, prominent in feasts and carnival, created for regeneration and birth (Bakhtin 1968). As the importance of the body as a vessel to truth increased, laughter culture also prospered. Laughter, pious or not so pious, flourished. It resided in the carnivalesque body, but was also introduced into the sacred presence of the suffering body of the saviour and the holy sacrament of bread and wine. The rebirth of classical ideals during the Renaissance brought with it not only a new interest in Aristotle's commentaries on laughter, but also in the dialogues of Lucian.[1] In philosophy there was a generally positive attitude toward laughter; its therapeutic value as a healing and regenerating element in life was especially stressed (Bakhtin 1968: 5–12).

As the popular feast and laughter culture flourished, the status and usefulness of laughter were again commented upon. The religious leaders of the late Middle Ages were more divided in their appraisal of laughter than their predecessors had been. Some maintained the traditional stand so often voiced in the early Church. One example is Petrus Cantor. To the question of whether Christ laughed, he answered that he could have done so, but one has not read that he did. In conformity with the Fathers of the early Church, he recommended only *mentis hilaritum*, spiritual joy (*Verbum abbreviatum*, 66). Laughter was still yoked to carnality. Hildegard of Bingen was convinced that the faculty of laughter was one of the consequences of the Fall of Man; had humans been perfect they would have voiced their higher joys in less carnal ways (Kolve 1966: 127).

Others were more broadminded and allowed kind mockery and mild mirth.[2] Thomas Aquinas, the great theologican of the Medieval Church, stretches the tolerance of the Church further than the Church Fathers of the fourth century had done in their treatment of laughter. In the second part of his *Summa Theologica*, Aquinas discusses three questions of relevance to the value of laughter: whether there can be a virtue about games; whether there can be sin in the excess of play; and whether there is sin in the lack of mirth. Aquinas appeals to the old 'experts' on laughter, such as Ambrose, Chrysostom and Aristotle, and concludes that it is lawful to make use of fun to relax the soul. He takes his cue from Aristotle and reintroduces the concept of *eutrapelia*, 'wittiness', which implies an ability to turn deeds or words toward relaxation, thus generating an attitude compatible with friendly and moderate joking. Aquinas even agrees with Aristotle that the lack of mirth is a vice. During the discussion, the positions of Jerome and Chrysostom are interpreted in ways that make them appear to be in harmony with the philosopher (*Summa Theologica*, qu. 168, art. 2–4). The result was that, without radically altering the traditional position of the Church, Aquinas interpreted laughter in a more positive vein than his predecessors.

However, much of the laughter culture that flourished so abundantly in these centuries under the Catholic Church would probably not have been deemed suitable by Aquinas. This culture included carnivals and festivals; theatrical performances in Latin and in the vernacular; and comical Latin texts parodying the holy scriptures as well as making fun of learned theological treatises and liturgies

(Bakhtin 1968: 11–18). The traditional elements of religion were brought into the material bodily sphere; the Gnostic position, spirit against matter, was reversed in the carnivalesque feasting inside and outside the church, in which the body was celebrated at the expense of the soul.

As in centuries before, the laughter of the late Medieval culture thrived on incongruities. Sources of laughter were the incongruity between the sublime soul and the material body with its processes of growth and decay, and the incongruity between the opulence and power of the Church and the ideal of evangelical poverty. These were often combined. Christian myth, ritual and priestly authority were infamously commented upon, for instance, in the Feast of Fools, a typical example of the late Medieval laughter culture. This feast created laughter which, perhaps for the first time in the history of the Church, happily celebrated the human body. It was a feast of the minor clerics held around Christmas in the churches of France.[3] The feast opened with a procession to the church, continued with Mass, developed into carnivals in the church and finally carnivals and theatrical performances outside the church. Thus, it started in solemnity and ended in burlesque. Its content was in no way fixed, but varied in the different churches and over the centuries. Originally only the subdeacons seem to have feasted, but over time, the lower clergy also participated in the fun.

THE FEAST OF FOOLS

That the Feast of Fools was celebrated as an opening up to the sensory world is explicitly reflected in the minor clerics' own apology for feasting, referred to in a letter from the Theological Faculty of Paris.[4] Here the inventive priests told the authorities that feasting is necessary because 'foolishness, which is our second nature and seems to be inherent in man, might freely spend itself at least once a year. Wine barrels burst if from time to time we do not open them and let in some air' (Bakhtin 1968: 75). They likened themselves to barrels, containers in which the wisdom of God fermented like wine. But according to the feasting priests, this fermenting was too violent to sustain without an opening up to the carnal world through the carnivalesque life.[5] To immerse oneself in jocularities and laughter had become a necessary indulgence for human beings.

The ecclesiastical authorities, on their side, did not like this feasting at all. In 1445, the Theological Faculty of Paris addressed a letter to the bishops and chapters of France. The letter sharply condemned the feast, which it says took place in different cathedrals and churches during Christmas and the New Year, and gives a colourful description of events:

> Priests and clerks may be seen wearing masks and monstrous visages at the hours of office. They dance in the choir dressed as women, panders or minstrels. They sing wanton songs. They eat black puddings at the horn of the altar while the celebrant is saying mass. They play at dice there. They cense with stinking smoke from the soles of old shoes. They run and leap through the church, without a blush at their own shame. Finally they drive about the town and its theatres in shabby traps and carts; and rouse the laughter of their fellows and the bystanders in infamous performances with indecent gestures and verses scurrilous and unchaste.[6]
>
> (Chambers 1954: 294)

The keynote of the feast was introduced for the first time in the Magnificat sung at Vespers. It proclaimed that the mighty were cast down from their seats and the low ones were exalted. This was the moment when the ceremonial staff (*baculus*), and probably a cope, were handed over to the leader of the subdeacons (Chambers 1954: 278). The staff and the cope were old symbols of power, and marked the authority of the one who now presided as the *dominus festi* and the importance of his group, the subdeacons or lower clergy. In the detailed letter from the Theological Faculty of Paris it is also stated that 'bishops' or 'archbishops' of Fools were chosen during the feast, and in churches under pontifical jurisdiction, even a pope was elected. A recurring trait of the feast is the use of ecclesiastical titles. Further, these 'bishops' and 'archbishops' wore 'mitres and pastoral staffs, and have crosses borne before them, as if they were on visitation'. They aped the duties of the clergy by performing the divine service and by giving benediction to the people.

During the feast, the regular church service was violated. The subdeacons left their stalls, ran and jumped about in the sanctuary, and danced round the altar. In Antibes, in the church of the Franciscans, the lay brothers held their books upside-down, wore spectacles made from orange peels and blew ashes from the censers at each other. They used the smoke from the soles of old shoes as incense, and played dice at the altar. In Beauvais, there was a drinking-bout in the portico.

The celebrants sang obscene songs (*cantilenas inhonestas*), distorting the words and the songs of the liturgy.[7] The priests were accused of dissonant singing, of gibberish, of shouting, hissing, howling, cackling and jeering. Both the answers of the celebrant and the people were sometimes distorted into braying. At St Omer, the whole office was recited at the highest pitch of the voice and with howls. The participants grimaced, used female clothes and wore flowers in their hair. Sometimes they turned their clothes inside out. There were even accusations that priests were appearing naked. Masks and monstrous visages recur in the sources.

Why did the feasting of the minor priests take this special form? On the one hand, these priests are indulging in a universal language of carnival. On the other hand, this comical performance and the laughter it generated gets its peculiar formulation from the priests' desire to comment upon the values of the Catholic Church – for instance the relationship between humans and animals, man and woman, high and low in the priestly hierarchy, body and soul.

The masks, for instance, were both of monsters and of animals. Their significance emerges in their contrast to the uniqueness of humans insisted upon in Christian anthropology: human beings stand in the middle position between God and animal, but are essentially different from both. In the feast, the religious goal of transcending biological nature and making it spiritual is reversed when humans appear as animals. In a similar way the structured liturgy is deconstructed, transformed into gibberish and animal noises. Thus, the movement from human to God is substituted by a movement from human to animal. Because an ass frequently stood in the centre of these celebrations, the feast was also called the 'Feast of Asses'.

In the context of the male Catholic hierarchy, in which the vestments of the priests are an important expression of their status, the feast's use of female clothes was meaningful. The traditional vestments of the priests transformed natural man and signified his aim of transcendence. Priests in female clothes were in comical contrast to the structures of hierarchy, to the spiritual emphasis on soul. The priestly vestments refer to Catholic ideology, including its ideal of celibacy. Female clothes, on the contrary, together with the clothes of panders and minstrels, have sexual connotations. In this connection the female represents disorder, nature and the body.[8] The erotic nature of the female and her role as a temptress is stressed, especially in a male society governed by the ideal of celibacy. The contrast between male and female is therefore also a contrast between asceticism and eroticism, highlighting an important aspect of the contrast between soul and body in Christian ideology.

The presence of the body was one of the most important features of the feast. One example is the 'censing' with old shoes. The early Church Fathers had forbidden incense in churches. But from the ninth century on, it was applied for the dedication and consecration of the altar. Incense serves a double purpose; it gives a pleasant smell and simultanously drowns out the smell of human bodies. The sweet fragrance points to a higher, unbodily reality. In contrast, censing with old shoes released a pungent stench of that low member of the human body, the foot.

This focus on the body also has a social reference. The material body is the human vehicle for being in the world. The body is what human beings have in common, the basic vehicle of communication in all types of interaction. The interaction created by feast and carnival is based on equality and not on status; participants are close and equal. There is accordingly a close correspondence between the rank of the social group in the feast and its preference for bodily symbols and sensory displays. In the Catholic hierarchy, the subdeacons were the *lowest* group. The *lowest* priests were always those who participated in the feast. They identified with the body as opposed to the soul and the spirit, which were associated with the higher priests.

When the. lower clergy played bishops, they were subdeacons in reality and bishops in appearance. In addition, these 'bishops' behaved like clowns. When the lower clergy used animal masks and made animal noises they were simultaneously humans and animals. The feast revelled in the play and juxtaposition of opposite meanings and of meanings pertaining to different spheres, a procedure which is most clearly seen in the feast's parody of traditional symbols. Religious carnivals make fun of traditional symbols and invent their own ludicrous symbols. In the Feast of Fools, the core symbol of the Catholic Church, the flesh and the blood of the saviour eaten in the Lord's Supper, was perverted, and a new core symbol, the Ass, was introduced.

DEFORMING THE LORD'S SUPPER AND ELEVATING THE ASS

In 1400, Gerson, Rector of the University of Paris, wrote this about the Feast of Fools: 'a detestable mockery is made of the service of the Lord and of the sacraments, where things are impudently and execrably done which should be done only in taverns and brothels, or among Saracens and Jews' (Swain 1932: 207).

The Theological Faculty of Paris especially forbade eating, drinking and dancing around the altar when the Mass was celebrated. Both in the Letter from the Theological Faculty and in one of the descriptions from Beauvais, the participants of the feast were accused of eating black pudding during the Mass. The letter says that priests and clerks 'eat black puddings at the horn of the altar while the celebrant is saying Mass'.[9] According to the manuscript from Beauvais, there was 'censing with pudding and sausage' on the day of the feast.[10]

The significance of the use of blood pudding and sausage in the feast rests in the significance of the Eucharist in the traditional Roman Mass. The Mass, the main cultic act of the Catholic Church, had developed into a dramatic performance centring around the consecration by the authorized priest of the bread and the wine as the body and blood of Christ. The result was twofold: it both supported a powerful priestly hierarchy within the Church and kindled the personal devotion of the individual worshipper:[11]

The new importance of the Eucharist was part of a general picture in which holiness received a new corporeal formulation. This formulation can be illustrated by the veneration of the relics of the saints, which took peculiar forms. For instance 'after Saint Thomas Aquinas had died in their monastery', the monks of Fossanuova 'in their fear of losing the relic, did not shrink from decapitating, boiling, and preserving the body' (Huizinga 1955: 168). The corporeal formulation of holiness was firmly linked to spiritual meanings. This was a delicate balance, a balance which could be upset when the material substance of the symbol was elevated at the expense of its spiritual meaning. In the Feast of Fools the symbol of bread and wine was interpreted literally, and its meaning became ludicrous. The ludicrous effect was obtained in the contrast between the values of the Catholic symbols and the new values created through their deformation. As the values of the Catholic symbols were turned

84

upside-down and made objects of subversive laughter, the power of the Catholic Church was also questioned.

During the feast, a hymn was sung in honour of the Ass.[12] According to the liturgy of Beauvais, both the celebrant and the congregation brayed like donkeys. Whether an ass was really led into the church or whether the animal was left standing outside the door of the church is not clear. However, its use as a symbol for the feast is established with certainty.

The Ass must be interpreted in the light of its two primary Biblical references: the prophetical Ass of Bileam in the Old Testament and the Ass on which Jesus rode into Jerusalem on Palm Sunday.[13] In iconography, the Ass is further represented in the Flight to Egypt, and at the crib of Jesus. The animal has a certain structuring effect by appearing both at the beginning and at the end of the life of Jesus. In churchly processions an ass frequently took part, most often acting the part of the Ass of Bileam or that of the Ass carrying the virgin and child to Egypt.[14] In short, in the Christian tradition, the Ass is a peaceful animal, appearing at important moments in the salvation history, but always playing a subordinate role.

In the Feast of Fools, all this is reversed. The Ass has moved into the foreground and even for a time plays the main role. In Christian mythology the Ass is part of the context. In the Feast of Fools it appears in focus (Bateson 1953, Fry 1963: 119). But when the Ass becomes the focus, its new position instantly affects the relationship between the other elements in the ideology of which it is a part. In all ideological systems, accentuation of one minor element changes the hierarchy and may eventually lead to its deconstruction. The elevation of the Ass implies a temporary change in the ideology and therefore a temporary change in the reality dependent on that ideology. A new perspective is created. This perspective – suggestive and implicit, transitory and ephemeral – is a jocular one. Like all jocular perspectives it is built upon the play of paradoxes.

In the new situation created by the Mass of the lower clergy, the Ass was simultaneously appropriate and extremely inappropriate. The Ass was, at the same time, both a Biblical animal and a natural animal: it was, undoubtedly a proper and peaceful Biblical ass, but it also activated another sphere of symbols with connotations outside the Biblical universe. In the different versions of the hymn to the Ass, the wavering between the Christian mythological sphere of the Ass and the natural sphere of the Ass is obvious.

This hymn alternates between past and present tense, and

between a description of and an address to the Ass. In this way the Ass is made symbolically present. Simultaneously the priest and the congregation mimicked its braying and thereby made it present as a menial beast. In the same way as the priest in the Mass varies between representing Christ, being an intermediary between God and man, and representing the congregation, the Ass acted both as subject and object. It was alternatively identified with the priest and with the congregation. In the congregation, the participants' individualities were submerged; a braying collective emerged. Simultaneously, the Ass of the song changed its braying into repeatedly saying *amen*. Thus the roles of human and animal were intentionally fused.[15] The dominant perspective, *the perspective of the Ass*, involved the continual changing of figure and ground, focus and fringe. Latent in this perspective was another sphere of connotations: according to current typologies of animals, the Ass was a stupid animal, connected with lust and with the body, regarded as unclean and generally held in low esteem. In other words, these notions are not rooted in Christian mythology, but in a classification of animals.

Primarily, the Ass referred to the subdeacons: the Ass was a domesticated animal, dominated as the subdeacons were dominated. In the same way as the subdeacons were low in the Church hierarchy, the Ass is low in the zoological hierarchy. Further, the stupidity of the Ass corresponded to the foolishness in the Feast of Fools. Nevertheless, the Ass was elevated in the Mass, as the subdeacons elevated themselves. The elevation of the Ass again activated the polarity in Christianity between human and beast. Universally, humans define their role in contrast to and in interplay with other beings. Christianity is an anthropocentric religion: human beings are superior to other living beings and shall legally rule over them as their steward. Humans are made in the image of God, but are never on the same level as Him. In this way human beings are fundamentally different both from God and from other animals. But human beings are also mediators between two poles of being, the animal and the divine, reflecting the duality of Christian anthropology. The tension between the angelic and the animal natures of humans is often interpreted as a tension between soul and body. The Ass is sometimes explicitly identified with the body. Its elevation is therefore the elevation of the beast and the body over Christ, the god/man, and over the spiritual dimension of being. As the bodily and the beastly are elevated to become the focus, the Mass itself is changed. So, in spite of its peaceful Biblical origin, the Ass paradoxically exposed a chaotic dimension of existence, representing a movement from the spiritual to the carnal. In short, the figure of the Ass concentrated the ludicrous meanings throughout the Feast of Fools, and therefore it is a fitting core symbol.

CARNIVAL IN RELIGION[16]

The Feast of Fools was nourished by the flourishing of a popular laughter culture in the late Middle Ages. A sort of happy acceptance of the materiality of the body seems to have characterized this carnivalesque celebration. What is equally interesting for us, however, is how the participants in this feast were invited systematically to laugh at the ideology and ritual of the Catholic Church. The minor priests derived no small part of their amusement from ludicrous parodies of the Mass, in which they made comical contrasts between the salvific flesh of the incarnated body of Christ and the material human body. The carnivalesque laughter was thus triggered by the contrast between two symbolic constructions of body, one expressed through the elaborated mythology and theology of the Catholic Church, the other through the grotesque bodily imagery of carnival, seen especially in the blood pudding and sausage and in the figure of the Ass.

The tensions of any cultural system put pressure on those involved – recall how the subdeacons likened themselves to barrels of fermenting wine. The priests exploited the tension present in the Catholic religious system, played with it and used it as 'fuel' for their feast. An alternative image to the fermenting wine in the barrels could, accordingly, be that of a balloon which is gradually filled with gas, then is let go to rush about in the air until it collapses on the ground. Just as with the balloon letting out gas, the movement of the feast, whirling and violent, released tension. It was as if the tension inherent in the Catholic religious system, which normally kept the elements of the religious system together, was let loose, increased and spent in a dynamic movement from form to lack of form. The priests feasted not only to let off steam and to relieve pressure, they also feasted to have fun. Without shame they *used* the pressure and the tension in the Catholic system for their own pleasure. Their feasting was not so much a release of a safety valve as it was a creative act.

The carnivalesque also has a social side. Carnival balances

between being a social criticism in disguise and being an instrument for social control. Applied to Medieval Christianity, this delicate balance – really, a tension of opposites – can be seen in the conflict between the ideal life of Christ and the real life of the Church, which was ventilated in the carnival of the fools. When the Feast of Fools flourished, the conflict was acute – there was a vivid consciousness of both the simple and egalitarian life lived by the apostles and the existence of a hierarchical Church with power, pomp and circumstance.

This conflict between the ideal and the real was also commented upon in other feasts; one example is the Feast of the Boy-bishop, in which a boy was treated as bishop and priests had to serve him. In this way the Christian ideal of the exalting of the low ones was expressed without threat to anyone's power. On the contrary, the feast contributed to the general benefit of the Church. In the Feast of Fools, the conflict between high and low, hierarchy and lack of hierarchy, ideal life versus real Church was ventilated more aggressively than in the Feast of the Boy-bishop, but in the end, the conflict was again made to seem harmless. While this conflict between the real and the ideal was one of the motivating powers of the feast, the priests took the sting out of their criticism by laughing and fooling around. The path from carnival to revolution was almost impassable when the impetus to revolt was drowned in feasting and merriment (Ladurie 1980).

CORPUS CHRISTI

The jocular commentaries of the priestly fools had their counterpart in the religious plays of England, in which laughter was more directly linked to the death of Christ and to his saving body, and served a more obvious religious purpose.

The cycles of English plays were originally a fruit of the Corpus Christi, the feast in which the symbolic Eucharistic world of the Medieval period culiminated. The host was carried through the streets of the towns in Europe, for everyone to adore.[17] In the wake of the feast, one of the most popular theatres the world has ever seen came into being. It existed from the fourteenth to the sixteenth century, and was in the main applauded by the Church. The plays of Corpus Christi comprised a cycle of twenty-five to fifty plays with such titles as *Fall of Lucifer*, *Creation of Adam and Eve*, *Noah's Flood*, *Shepherds' Play*, *Crucifixion* and *Judgement*.[18] Through their daring comical exploitation of divine flesh, these plays demonstrate an absolute confidence in the salvific power of that flesh.

In these plays, the Christian drama of salvation was carried out on portable stages set up on wagons especially decorated for the occasion. The players were amateurs. Different guilds were responsible; each presented one play, often of special relevance to its craft.[19] Between two hundred and four hundred of the inhabitants of Chester, York, Wakefield and other towns had speaking parts, and they did not shrink from playing God or the Devil.[20]

Mythology and reality were intermingled on these portable stages of Medieval England: in many cases the craftsmen of the guilds made their craft into a special gateway to the holy mysteries. The borderlines between Bethlehem and York became blurred and it was difficult to tell the shepherds of Galilee from those of Yorkshire. This contributed to making the plays seem contemporary, but also allowed certain episodes to seem anachronistic and comic. The plays did not hesitate to exhibit the most sacred parts of religion, transform them into comedy and make people laugh.[21]

Similar to Dante's *Divina Comedia*, the tenor of the cycles was comic. They started with creation, were followed by the fall of Lucifer and of Adam and Eve, dwelt on the tragedy of the Passion, but ended with the joy of resurrection and salvation. A few of the individual plays were tragic (for instance *Sacrifice of Cain and Abel*, *Slaughter of the Innocent*, *Crucifixion*). But because the audience knew that the tragedy was only apparent and incidental, the tragic plays were acted out in comical contrast to the overall cycle. Even the tragic plays were punctuated with episodes intended to make the audience laugh, for instance when Cain nearly chokes because God sends the smoke from his sacrifice straight back into his face; when Noah is bullied by his formidable wife; when Joseph behaves as a suspicious cuckold; or when King Herod rages and raves (Kolve 1966: 124–74, Hotchkiss, 1965, Shershow 1986: 104–15, Wood 1940). Some of the comic episodes are directly related to the major themes of Christian mythology, most famously in *The Second Shepherds' Play* from Wakefield, connected with the birth of Jesus':[22] But comic scenes are also found even in connection with the torturing and crucifixion of Jesus in several plays from all the cycles. In both the nativity and the crucifixion scenes the religious challenge posed by the divine body with its human flesh is exploited in a comical manner.

The Second Shepherds' Play

The most famous of the English mystery plays is *The Second Shepherds' Play*, written in the sixteenth century by a writer known as the Wakefield Master (Woolf 1984, Helterman 1981, Staines 1991: 90). Its Biblical theme is the shepherds and the nativity. The plot is based on the contrast – but also the connection – between a stolen lamb laid in a crib and passed off as a newborn child, and the child Jesus, the lamb of God who carries the sins of the world.

The thief who stole the sheep is called Mak. When the shepherds discover the theft, they accuse Mak. Mak has put the lamb in a crib passing it off as his newborn son. He stubbornly maintains that he has no lamb, and his wife, Gill, swears that if she has fooled them, she shall 'eat this child that lies in this cradle' (T 14, 537–8)[23] The shepherds show their interest in this 'child' and want to give him something, 'that little day-starn' (T 14, 577). But when one of the shepherds lifts him up to kiss him, he glimpses the sheep: 'What the devil is this? He has a long snout!' (T 14, 585). Suddenly he realizes that it is their own stolen sheep:

> Will ye see how they swaddle
> His four feet in the middle?
> Saw I never in a cradle
> A horned lad ere now.
> (T 14, 598–601)

Mak and Gill do not give in; they claim first that it is a child, and then, when the shepherds do not believe them, they claim the child is deformed. Eventually they insist that they have got a changeling from the elves. The shepherds threaten to kill Mak and Gill, but content themselves with tossing Mak about in a blanket.

After having rescued their lamb, the shepherds go to sleep. But they are awakened by the song of an angel with the command to go to Bethlehem to greet the newborn saviour. Full of joy and wonder the shepherds set out, reminding each other of the prophecies about this saviour. In Bethlehem they greet the laughing child, and give him cherries, a bird and a ball: 'Have and play thee withal, and go to the tennis' (T 14, 735–6).

In *The Second Shepherds' Play*, the playwright used the simple comical technique of incongruity when he contrasted Mak's stolen lamb with the divine child (Woolf 1972: 188). The structure of this comical plot is universal; the two birth-scenes reflect each other as in a distorting mirror. The play probably evoked special laughter in York, where sheep farming was an important livelihood.

An abundance of comical paradoxes were created because of the relevance of the lamb to the Christian universe. Mak's 'son' was a lamb, but lying in the cradle with horns and snout, in one moment appearing as both man and animal, he was rather a devil's brat. Mak himself was the evil shepherd, turning the narrative of the good shepherd on its head. In contrast to the Biblical shepherd who saved the one sheep, he stole one sheep out of its flock to eat it and behaved, as the dream of the shepherds suggested, as a wolf. The real sacrificial lamb was Christ, *Agnus Dei*, who carried the sins of the world. Gill swore that she would eat Mak's son if the shepherds found the lamb, and thus made a connection between the newborn 'child' and the Lord's Supper (cf. lines 522, 537, 555–6). This connection is repeated at the end of the play when one of the shepherds indicates that he will drink the blood of the Christ-child: [24]

> Of our creed thou art crop;
> I would drink on thy cop,
> Little day-starn.
> (T 14, 725–7)

The creative tension at the heart of the Eucharist symbol received comic treatment through the Wakefield Master's art with its web of connections and oppositions between the lamb and the Son of God, food and Host, slaughter and divine sacrifice, Gill and Mak and the holy family, the evil shepherd and the good shepherd. Some critics have suggested that when Mak appeared with his travesties of the Lord's Supper and his parody of the gospel for Christmas day, he represented an incarnation of Satan, and indeed many of the villains in the Wakefield cycle have certain satanic qualities. This is probably to take him far too seriously, though; at most he was a clown who foolishly played the devil (Helterman 1981: 95–114). *The Second Shepherds' Play* was pious comedy, but had some blasphemous subnotes which contributed to the fun. Those subnotes, however, were never allowed to get in the way of the main purpose of the play, which was to give a vivid representation of the Biblical narrative, to make its events contemporary and present, and finally to show the great design of salvation of which these events were part.

In *The Second Shepherds' Play*, though the nameless Wakefield Master used his comical skill to create a special plot with Eucharistic jokes and paradoxes,[25] he did not break with the traditional structure and purpose of the plays. Rather he made that structure and purpose more visible. The Corpus Christi feast was a celebration of the Eucharist; the mystery plays were a special celebration of that sacrament, staging the whole salvation story and stressing how it had altered the destiny of humanity (Kolve 1966: 48–9). When the Wakefield Master created a parody of the Eucharist, he was commenting upon the main theme of the Corpus Christi feast.[26]

In the play, the contrast between the body of the child Jesus and the stolen sheep was a comical contrast between flesh which is salvific and flesh which is merely flesh. This is a contrast found in other plays as well. At the heart of Christian doctrine in the later Medieval period was the Passion of Christ and the Lord's Supper. Events and persons in the Old Testament together with the lives of martyrs and saints were often viewed as *figura* of Passion and Eucharist, i.e., they either pointed forward to Christ or were preceded by him. The Christian universe was thus filled with a web of relationships and connections.

Jesus, Mary, the Host, the saints and the relics incarnated spirit in the world. The contrast between the physical connotations of flesh and its spiritual connotations, made visible and comic in *The Second Shepherds' Play*, is seen in different variants in the cycles. In the events immediately preceeding the nativity in the cycle from N-town, the contrast is most irreverently present in the comical presentation of Joseph as a cuckold in the play named after him. But more seriously, in *The Nativity*, the contrast between physical and spiritual flesh appears as a theological point in the midwives' gynaecological examination of Mary.[27] And the contradiction of mortal flesh and divine flesh is abundantly present in the climax of the cycles, the Passion and crucifixion of Christ. The comic fantasy does not shrink from exploiting this important object of piety in late Medieval culture (Rubin 1991).

Crucifixio Christi

Because the Passion and the crucifixion were at the centre of Christian mythology, ritual and piety, they were of special relevance for the Corpus Christi feast, and were the subject of several plays in each cycle. These plays presupposed a twofold emotional reception from the audience: the suffering of Christ was played realistically and the audience was invited to see and feel the intense suffering of

Christ and its effects on his broken body. But their participation in the experience was controlled and limited because, unlike the 'soldiers' and 'torturers' on the scenes, the audience knew that the ultimate outcome of the crucifixion was salvation. That knowledge made it possible for the playwrights to hold the soldiers and torturers up to ridicule and to incorporate genuinely comical episodes (Kolve 1966: 199). Thus suffering and grief were held in check by comedy. The comedy was played out in two ways: either it appeared as a simple contrast between the soldiers' and torturers' utterly material approach to the suffering body of Jesus versus the divinity of that body, or it appeared as a more complicated contrast between the sadistic games the soldiers were playing versus the divine game that was played with them. Both approaches are found in combination in the Passion plays. When it comes to the crucifixion plays, Wakefield includes sadistic games of mockery while in the Chester and N-town cycles the dramatization is more modest. York is the most realistic.

In York, the four soldiers approach the crucifixion in the spirit of self-confident craftsmen.[28] For them the crucifixion is primarily a job. They are anxious that nothing should go wrong and have 'Both hammers and nails large and long' ready when they start their work (Y 35, 30). But they are confronted with bad workmanship. To begin with, the holes in the cross have been drilled in the wrong places: 'it fails a foot and more' (Y 35,107), so they fasten a rope to the limbs of Jesus and start to pull: 'A rope shall rug him down, If all his sinews go asunder' (Y 35, 131–2). They care nothing for the suffering of their victim:

> 1. Soldier: These cords have evil increased his pains,
>   Ere he were till the borings brought.
> 2. Soldier: Yea, asunder are both sinews and veins
>   On ilka side, so have we sought.
> (Y 35,145–8)

When it comes to lifting the cross, carrying it to its place, and raising it, the soldiers complain loudly in contrast to the silence of Jesus, 'He weighs a wicked weight' (Y 35, 213).[29] When at last they have got the cross in place and are about to let it go, the fourth soldier says, 'Let down, so all his bones/are asunder nown on sides sere' (Y 35, 223–4), and the first soldier comments in passing on the terrible pain they have just given their victim when they let go of the cross. Still, they have not managed to get the cross standing, and they start to work on it with wedges and hammers. When finally Jesus comments on his pain and on the sacrifice he has made on behalf of humankind, the soldiers neither understand nor show any sympathy. On the contrary, they start to draw lots for his coat and finally leave the place.

In this play, the soldiers treat the body of Jesus as an object of their trade, a thing which raises technical questions they have to solve, not a human being. But the craftsmen do poor work; their skills are not much to boast about. The fact that the actors who played the soldiers were carpenters and painters in real life and would know a thing or two about nails, hammers, ropes and wedges, would have created a comical effect for the contemporary viewing audience.[30]

Unlike the torturers in the York play, the torturers in the Wakefield *Crucifixion* conceive of the crucifixion as a game they are playing with Jesus:

> Now we are at the Mount of Calvary,
> Have done, fellows, and let now see
> How we can with him play.
>
> (T 23, 83–5)

The gospels tell how the soldiers 'played' with Jesus before he was crucified. He was blindfolded, beaten and asked to guess who it was that had beaten him. The soldiers ridiculed Jesus and clothed him in the shrouds of a mock king, with a purple coat, a reed in his hand and a crown of thorns on his head. After he had been hung on the cross, they threw dice to determine who would get his clothes. The mystery plays continued this tradition of mocking 'games' but went further than the gospels. At the Passion, the soldiers and torturers joke while they are 'working' and introduce new 'games' not found in the gospels.[31]

In the Wakefield *Crucifixion*, the torturers pretend that they prepare a knight for a tournament, put him in his saddle and make him ride a horse. They find this very funny because, in their view, the role of the knight contrasts radically with the reality of the tortured prisoner. As in the York play, the torturers stretch out the limbs of Jesus with a rope, and are very pleased with themselves ('That was well drawn out, that', T 23,144) but start to quarrel about whether they are all pulling equally or whether someone is making it easy for himself. Unlike their York contemporaries, the Wakefield actors actively enjoy what they are doing, turning it into sadistic fun. When

Jesus speaks from the cross, he concludes with the ominous words. 'They know not what they doon,/Nor whom they thus have spoilt!' (T 23, 293–4). The first torturer immediately replies, 'Yes, what we do full well we know' (T 23, 295), and thereby shows his ignorance. At this point the torturers get impatient. They lift the cross and let it fall, so that Jesus will die faster. The terrible state of the body of Jesus is commented upon by Mary and John in moving speeches, and also by Jesus: 'Blue and bloody thus am I beat,/Swongen with swepys and all a-sweat' (T 23, 469–70).

Up to his death the torturers continue with their mockeries. In the end they trick a blind knight, Longeus – known from apocryphal legends – to pierce Jesus' side with a spear, to see if Jesus really is dead. Because of his blindness Longeus does not understand what they have made him do, but the act, made in innocence and followed by repentance, lets him miraculously regain his sight. In the end, the broken body of Jesus is taken down by Joseph and Nicodemus.

Two levels of comedy work together in the crucifixion plays, producing a synergistic effect. Within the play, the comic action takes place between the actors in the form of horrible sadistic fun. Between the play and the audience, a contrast is made between the soldiers' sport and 'fun' acted out against the vulnerable body, and the audience's better knowledge about the absolute significance this tortured body has for the salvation of human beings. The synergism is produced because it really *is* the torturing and crucifixion of the saviour that stands at the centre of the Christian mystery of salvation. In this way, the internal level of sadistic games and cruel torture 'fertilizes' the second level of the audience's understanding and increases the comic effect.

The comedy of the crucifixion plays lies in a special conception of the body, in which the human flesh has a deep religious significance as an instrument for salvation (Richardson and Johnston 1991: 77–8, Ashley 1979). Unlike the Gnostics, who made a dualistic point by playing out the spiritual body against the material, the Corpus Christi plays situated jokes in the opposition between the conception of the body as mortal flesh and the body as immortal – the carrier of the human soul. In Corpus Christi, the laughter of the audience proves that they have seen the point; their laughter matches the opening of Longeus' eyes when he pierces the side of Jesus with the spear. In stark contrast to the Gnostic myths in which the violent opening up of the body led nowhere, the opening up of the body of Jesus was an act of salvation. It led to an opening up of blind eyes, and in Corpus Christi, to liberating laughter.

EMBODIED LAUGHTER

The meaning of the comic in the Corpus Christi plays has been extensively debated. Laughter has been seen as something vulgar and external to the religious content of the plays, or as marginal to the plays' superior religious purpose. There has been a reasonable consensus, however, that the laughter of the audience was a weapon against evil.

It is easy to agree with the last point of view: evil was given a face through the Devil, demons and fallen angels. Evil was not reduced or explained away. On the contrary, the experience of evil was personified. The Corpus Christi plays are swarming with scoundrels, big and small: Satan and Lucifer and their demonic helpers; Judas, Annas, Caiphas, Herod and Pilate; soldiers and torturers. Some of them loved evil for evil's sake and were terribly wicked; others were evil because of ignorance. The worst of the human scoundrels was Herod, but even if his mad wickedness knew no limits, he was at the same time cast as a comic figure, just as many of the other scoundrels often were. Laughter thus took the sting out of evil and reduced the champions of wickedness to raving and raging fools. When the audience laughed at the demons and human scoundrels, they laughed from their position of superior knowledge. Thus, the comedy of the Corpus Christi plays appears as both religious and pious.

But even if the comic in the plays fights on the side of good against evil, the laughter of the audience was not simply a pious laughter. The plays were not restricted to poking fun at the devil and his servants; laughter was also provoked by cruelty and sadism and was clearly situated in the unstable space created by the paradox of the divine incarnation, as seen in *The Second Shepherds' Play* and *The Crucifixion* from York and Wakefield.

The Eucharist is a key to this paradoxical space. The theological position of the Eucharistic symbol, verbalized by Thomas Aquinas, with his distinction between *accidentia* and *substantia*,[32] opened up to a type of symbolic thinking which was characteristic of Christianity in the late Middle Ages. As a key symbol, the Eucharist continually generated power by means of the tension between its sensory and ideological poles.[33] The desires and emotions awakened by the sensory pole – human flesh and blood – were kept in check by this flesh and blood being mediated through the small wheaten disc and the wine. But when the incarnation and the Eucharist are the subjects of comedy and laughter, the interpretation of them is no longer fully contained. The boxes into which theology and dogma have put the most uncomfortable connotations of god made flesh and blood, tortured, killed and eaten, are suddenly opened. From these boxes arise connotations with cannibalism and sadism which account for much of the comedy connected with the nativity and the crucifixion of Christ (Prosser 1961: 84; Hotchkiss 1965: 72). The Corpus Christi plays show a great capacity for holding these different perspectives in tension, and creating ludicrous meanings through a play upon them.

In the plays, both a derisive laughter striking at evil and a more complicated creative laughter playing on the corporality and doubleness of central Christian symbols are present. Laughter is drawn into the sphere of the violated divine body, which in this late phase of Medieval Christianity had become a profound source of religious meaning. The traditional position of the Catholic Church, according to which the human soul is sanctified by means of the vulnerable body, is celebrated in the Corpus Christi plays.

If we compare the laughter of the Corpus Christi and the laughter of the Feast of Fools with reference to their use of bodily symbolism, we find that in the Feast of Fools, the material body is contrasted with the divine flesh of the saviour. Sausages and blood pudding have replaced the Eucharist, the Ass rules supreme, the subdeacons are fooling around. Laughter has clearly taken its stand with the material body. In the Corpus Christi plays, however, the direction of laughter is different and its basis is more complicated. In these plays the incarnated body of the saviour is contrasted with a conception of the body as material and perishable. In other words, the obvious, realistic explanation of body is overruled by the religious interpretation, and a comic contrast is made between the two, a move which shows great confidence in the salvific power of Jesus' human flesh. This confidence was so absolute that it could be exposed to joking and unrestrained laughter. In other words, while the Feast of Fools indulged in a comic celebration of the human body, the laughter of the Corpus Christi celebrated the belief in the saving flesh of the divine body against a non-salvific conception of that flesh. In the Feast of Fools, the body, connected to the processes of growth and decay, was celebrated; in the Corpus Christi plays the great paradox of the salvific power inherent in corruptible flesh was praised.

Compared to the early Church, it is striking how religious laughter in the late Medieval period has moved out of mythological texts and monastic rules and appears in the middle of the life of the Church. In a sense, this development is reasonable. It is probably no coincidence that the examples of spiritual laughter from the early Church were textual, while examples of the embodied laughter of the late Middle Ages are taken from practices. The impulse to laugh in the Middle Ages was no longer censored as it was in the early Church with its battle against the body. Nor was laughter, as in Gnostic religion, used to lay bare the polarity of soul and body. Taken together, these examples reflect a development in the Christian history of laughter from laughter being singled out as an object for restrictions to it being fostered through religious theatres and feasts. Could, perhaps, this development be connected with a development in the religious approach to the body? In the early Church it seems to have been a goal to make the perishable body static and unchangeable by means of a rigid discipline, as we saw, for instance, with the virgins of Jerome and the desert monks. Then laughter was only permitted when it reflected the superior state of incorruptibility. However, the processual character of laughter, its eruptivity and its connection with sexuality, made it in general too firmly linked to the biological organism of fertility and decay to be compatible with the holy life.

A thousand years later, when the Corpus Christi cycles were played in the towns of England and the Feast of Fools was celebrated in the churches of France, the focus had changed. By the thirteenth and the fourteenth centuries, a preoccupation with the corruptibility and changeability of the body was in evidence (Bynum 1995). It is seen, for instance, in how the body of Christ was shown as bleeding and suffering and in the veneration of the fragments of the bodies of the saints, but also in the practice of judical torture on living bodies and in how dead bodies were partitioned for religious or medical purposes. It is as if the corruptibility which is inherent in bodies was fully revealed; they were opened up; their interior was investigated; they were fragmented. One dared to look into all the gruesome details of wounded, tortured, mutilated and rotting bodies and still proclaim their final resurrection when God would triumph over all bodily decay. When bodily imagery becomes more concrete and more concentrated upon the mortal flesh, the body

laughter became generally critical and restrictive. Laughter still sat in the body, perhaps more so than ever before. But the eruptive sides of bodily life were not revealed in public, and uncontrolled outbursts of laughter were condemned as vulgar by the upper classes. The words of Lord Chesterfield from the mid-eighteenth century are famous: 'There is nothing so illiberal, and so illbred, as audible laughter' (Thomas 1977: 80). Because the body in Western tradition was degraded in relation to the soul, laughter with its anchorage in the body was also devalued against superior reason. After the Renaissance, the image of body as a machine was current. This way of looking at the body led to new ways of thinking about it. In a continuation of this thinking, laughter frequently became treated and explained as merely a physiological phenomenon.

In the twentieth century, however, there has been a fundamental reassessment of laughter, a reassessment which is so widespread that it is tempting to talk about a new turning point in the Western history of laughter. This turning point is perhaps even more far-reaching than that which took place from the end of the sixteenth to the seventeenth century: theories of humour in the twentieth century are almost uniformly positive in their evaluation of laughter, regarding it as a means to make human beings whole and in harmony with their bodies and with society. Part of the explanation of why laughter now receives such a positive evaluation is that it is mostly viewed in relation to humour, and modern theories of humour have concentrated on the perception of incongruity. The ability to perceive incongruities is considered to be a hallmark of the human mind. Because incongruity is more and more seen as the one all-encompassing feature present when most laughter is triggered off, the ludicrous is to an increasing degree viewed in relation to the mind. Consequently laughter becomes a cerebral phenomenon and a sign pointing to the rationality of human beings. In other words, laughter has moved from the body to the brain. Being associated with the highest skills of human beings has considerably increased laughter's general significance. How this new status also affects laughter's relationship to religion will be the topic of the next chapters.

6

MODERNITY AND THE REMYTHOLOGIZATION OF LAUGHTER
Churchly boredom and therapeutic laughter

As we have noted before, religion is traditionally regarded as a matter of ultimate concerns. But in Western societies today, even if religion is concerned with ultimate matters, it also exists as a superficial phenomenon, and it has a great entertainment potential. Religious themes, symbols and narratives are taken up in novels, films, and popular magazines throughout the so-called secularized world. And as religion has been made part of entertainment, it is also demanded that religion shall be entertaining – one new criterion for modern religion is that it keeps one amused. On that basic principle 'televangelism' is built, to mention but one example (Postman 1993).

Thus, in modern Western societies, religious aspects of laughter are incorporated into twentieth-century secular culture, and laughter is introduced into contemporary religious culture. This new interplay between religion and laughter is found in modern novels and scientific literature, as well as in theological treatises and religious practice. Underneath all these examples lies a conception of laughter where it is seen as a positive contributor to human liberation, spiritual growth and wisdom. Laughter relieves tension, vanquishes rigidity and helps to cultivate a playful attitude toward life. *Homo ludens* is celebrated as one of the ideals of this century, and laughter has become a ticket to the lost paradise of play.

This new significance given to laughter and the playful element of life is, for instance, supported by the psycho-literary tradition. This tradition has explored the body through literature and psychoanalysis as an object and agent of desire, hidden in narrative and language. Its roots lay in Sigmund Freud's reading of culture.

According to his Relief theory, jokes are seen as safety valves for forbidden thoughts and feelings, especially of sexuality and violence; they are keys to secrets hidden at the depths of human existence. The body is made to speak through its laughter and laughter in its turn invites interpretation.

In the extension of the Freudian and psycho-literary tradition, contemporary feminist writers have created a new *female* space for laughter with specifically regenerative and religious connotations: Julia Kristeva stresses the female dimension of language and narrative as a deep rhythm and hidden space which creates laughter (Kristeva 1980: 280–6), while Hélène Cixous introduces the laughing Medusa as a symbol for the open, overflowing, laughing bodies of women (Cixous 1976).

Such examples from twentieth-century intellectual culture suggest a general tendency to include concepts, images and references taken from religion and mythology when describing the positive value of laughter. Two influential books – Mikhail Bakhtin, *Rabelais and his World*, and Umberto Eco, *The Name of the Rose* – have contributed especially to the creation of the modern mythology of laughter. They illustrate how well this mythology fits with modernity and, more generally, how important religious themes remain in our culture, even when they are detached from religious institutions. It is therefore useful to examine these books in greater detail.

BAKHTIN AND UTOPIAN LAUGHTER

In *Rabelais and his World*, written by the Russian semiotician Mikhail Bakhtin in 1940, and translated into English in 1968, a mythology of laughter is fully developed. Here carnival laughter is virtually made an alternative to religion and presented as the true exponent of the folk culture of the Middle Ages. The theme of Bakhtin's book is the connection between Rabelais' Renaissance novel and the Medieval laughter culture. At the book's centre stands the carnival and the material body, which is conceived in terms of food, drink, defecation and sexual life. The carnivalesque body is not expressed in any individual body, but in the collectivity of the people. It is pictured as an enormous grotesque, characterized by brimming abundance, always opening up to the world, at the same time swallowing up and giving birth:

We repeat: the body and bodily life have here a cosmic and at the same time an all-people's character; this is not the body and its physiology in the modern sense of these words, because it is not individualized. The material bodily principle is contained not in the biological individual, not in the bourgeois ego, but in the people, a people who are continually growing and renewed. This is why all that is bodily becomes grandiose, exaggerated, immeasurable.

(Bakhtin 1968: 19)

The openings in the body are especially significant. What sort of meanings do the openings of the Bakhtinian body lead to? These meanings are connected with the body's physiological processes and with the satisfaction of primary needs. Though the explicit connection between bodily openings and laughter had been made early in Christianity, at that time, this connection was regarded as disturbing and a reason to curb laughter. Radically new in Bakhtin is how the connection between laughter, the carnivalesque body and bodily openings are elaborated in a positive direction and develop existential meaning.

One of Bakhtin's concerns was to establish the significance of laughter as a cultural force. This laughter of carnival is cast in the Middle Ages, but is, perhaps, more a product of the thinking about laughter of the twentieth century. Bakhtin's carnival laughter is moulded in opposition to the ruling conception of laughter in the eighteenth and nineteenth centuries; the bodily laughter of carnival is no longer a negative and rather insignificant expression. On the contrary, Bakhtin describes laughter as cathartic and salvific, an expression of rebellion aimed at the religious authorities and their institutions, past and present. According to him, the forms and rituals based on laughter had systematically been placed outside the life of the Church, officialdom and politics. Laughter belonged to another world: 'Thus carnival is the people's second life, organized on the basis of laughter. It is a festive life. Festivity is a peculiar quality of all comic rituals and spectacles of the Middle Ages' (Bakhtin 1968: 8). The carnival feasts of the people looked into the future, to a utopian realm of community characterized by freedom, equality and abundance, in contrast to the ecclesiastical feasts, whose main function was to sanction the existing order. Traditional and static Christianity was opposed to such carnivalesque elements of change and renewal.

The construction of the carnivalesque body and its laughter is of course a reaction to the Age of Reason with its subduing of the physical and bodily aspects of reality. Bakhtin brings the body back in force, and introduces carnival laughter, characterized by its ability to degrade and materialize the more subtle elements of culture. Such laughter always points downward, from high to low, from spirit to body, from head to genitals and buttocks. In short, it is the festive laughter of the people, as Bakhtin puts it:

> Let us say a few initial words about the complex nature of carnival laughter. It is, first of all, a festive laughter. Therefore it is not an individual reaction to some isolated 'comic' event. Carnival laughter is the laughter of all the people. Second, it is universal in scope; it is directed at all and everyone, including the carnival's participants. The entire world is seen in its droll aspect, in its gay relativity. Third, this laughter is ambivalent: it is gay, triumphant, and at the same time mocking, deriding. It asserts and denies, it buries and revives. Such is the laughter of carnival.
>
> (Bakhtin 1968: 11–12)

When Bakhtin describes the evolutionary development of the laughter culture of Europe, in which laughter goes from a golden age to an age of fall, and contrasts pagan culture with the seriousness of Christianity, laughter becomes an expression of a salvific generative power. And even if this generative power had been subdued by Christianity, it is universal, collective and never exclusive. Bakhtin's underlying, utopian goal is to restore humans to the regenerative and transforming realm of laughter. But this realm is a paradise lost, impossible to reach within the modern world. Because it thus remains a carnivalesque fantasy, no longer obtainable in social forms, its recapture is possible only through art.[1]

Bakhtin, through his conception of carnival, ascribes religious significance to laughter. His interpretation of religion and history was not only indebted to anthropological thinking of his time, but also to a nostalgic view of modernity which looked back to an earlier time, when meaning was created through participation in and repetition of a ritual/festival calendar. This nostalgic dwelling on the past reminds us not only of the famous work of James Frazer, *The Golden Bough* (Børtnes 1993: 122), but also of a younger contemporary of Bakhtin, Mircea Eliade, the most well-known historian of religions in the second half of this century, a scholar who has been described as 'the seal of the prophets in that religion or tradition known as "The History of Religion(s)" and, after him, the canon is closed' (Corless 1993: 373).

Bakhtin and Eliade shared a view of modernity as a fall, and both wrote texts in which they recreated what they perceived as a lost universe of wholeness and meaning. But where Eliade looked for divine, cosmic transcendence, Bakhtin praised the immanent universal body as the great cosmic principle. In place of dying gods and sacrifices, Bakhtin emphasizes rituals of carnival and laughter.

If we cast a critical eye on Bakhtin's description of religion in the Middle Ages, though, his description is not quite convincing. For instance, when Bakhtin draws a picture of Medieval religion, he describes festival laughter too strictly in opposition to the ruling religious culture. The feasts of the people and the feasts of the Church were not so distinctive from each other, nor could the division between body and soul be conceived of in an absolute dualistic perspective (cf. chapter 5). On the contrary, and as we have already seen, the body in Catholic Christianity was a means to reach the soul and it was an object of salvation. Yet Bakhtin vividly portrayed a utopian laughter of carnival and the body. Why had the Middle Ages become an ideal? Why did this sudden apotheosis of the trinity of laughter, carnival and the body appear? What was its significance?

One reason for the glorification of the Middle Ages was probably a certain agreement between the modern and the Medieval – certain points where they converged. Such convergences emerged in the mutual interest these two periods had in semiotics, hierarchy, religion and the body. Medieval culture was a society of signs, with complex theories about these signs' interconnection and manners of operation. When Bakhtin investigated the codes of Medieval feasts and carnival through Rabelais' novel, he bridged the distance between the old culture of signs and its modern counterpart, semiotics. But probably more important than semiotics for Bakhtin's investigation was Bakhtin's own historical situation – the opposition between the Communists and the elite during the 1920s and 1930s. Later, when his book appeared in the United States, Bakhtin's construction of polar oppositions in Medieval culture – between high and low, hierarchy and the folk, soul and body – found a resounding echo in the opposition between the US counterculture and the Establishment in the 1960s. In America, Bakhtin's work on carnival was very well received by those who were influenced by ideals of free love, community and equality.

These ideals countered the rationalizing tendency of Western thought, with its taming of affect and emotion, its regulation and mechanization of the body. Bakhtin's book on Rabelais can be regarded as a great utopian attempt to reclaim the body amidst all the modern forces which had gradually led to subduing the body. Bakhtin sought to establish the body as the ultimate signifier, and to make laughter its key symbol. Thus, Bakhtin created a significant symbolic connotation for laughter in the late twentieth century – the human body as a mythological construction.

But Bakhtin's conception of the body in no way bridges the split between mind and body in Western thinking. On the contrary, it rather presupposes and continues that split. For even if Bakhtin makes an apotheosis of the body, this body still remains opposed to the mind and rationality. The fact that Bakhtin chose laughter as the preferred expression of the bodily material principle is typical of laughter's position in late modernity, which is rather paradoxical: on the one hand, laughter is treated as a phenomenon of the mind, thus giving it a new status. On the other hand, in Bakhtin's mythological context, laughter is a symbol of the life in the body, thus making laughter a seemingly simple channel into an immensely complex reality. Laughter becomes utopian.

POSTMODERN MYTHOLOGY

Bakhtin's carnivalesque fantasy has been very influential. His influence is, for instance, seen in Umberto Eco's *The Name of the Rose* (1980). Eco's novel is also set in the conflict between the Middle Ages and the Renaissance, has a constitutive semiotic perspective and has oppositional laughter as a main theme. We could indeed say that Umberto Eco wrote *the* book about religion and laughter for the 1980s. But Eco's work, *The Name of the Rose* is not literary criticism, but a novel, and, more important, its concept of laughter is no longer anchored primarily in the body.

The Name of the Rose is a Medieval whodunit, set in a monastery where strange murders occur. The open-minded Brother William of Baskerville, accompanied by the young Adso of Melk, has been sent for to investigate the murders. William's antagonist is the old monk Jorge, who is in charge of the monastery's precious library. No one has access to the library except Jorge, who jealously guards its secrets. What secrets? In several discussions between Jorge and William, laughter turns up as a topic. Jorge is an opponent of laughter, and refers to John Chrysostom, Petrus Cantor and the tradition that

Jesus never laughed. He consistently reflects a negative attitude to laughter, partly supported by the texts of the Christian Fathers. Inside the library, this sinister monk has hidden away the second part of Aristotle's *Poetics*. Jorge sees this book as especially dangerous because it praises the liberating potential of laughter. What Jorge cannot tolerate is that, through this possibly fictive work of Aristotle, laughter is removed from association with the low, the drunk and fools, and honoured with philosophical value. If the existence of this Aristotelian book became known, the status of laughter would be completely reversed, and that would have meant an upheaval of religious tradition. Because he is fanatical in his wish to open up neither the library to visitors, nor his closed Medieval universe to liberation and laughter, Jorge becomes a murderer.

The Aristotelian laughter is set free from its confinement in the library by an apocalyptic blast of fire which devours the monastery. Eco's book is not so much about laughter *per se*: laughter is put within a system of signs in a true semiotic project which is an intellectual enterprise cast as a detective novel. When at the end of the novel the book is destroyed, the reader realizes that no ultimate signifier exists.

The transition of the position of laughter from Bakhtin's text to Eco's novel can be described as the transition from modern to postmodern. While Bakhtin recovers the codes of carnival and argues for the revival of laughter through literature and art, Eco posits laughter as a sign, a part of a puzzle, a phenomenon of the mind. In Eco's work, laughter no longer points to the meaning of the body, but to the transitory play of the mind. Laughter becomes a triumph of the intellect when the solution of the crime puzzle is revealed. It is probably unnecessary to say that academicians loved *The Name of the Rose*.

Both Bakhtin and Eco chose to anchor laughter in a text of revelation, be it Rabelais or Aristotle. And what else is there to anchor the idea of laughter in than in a text? While laughter still has a positive, cathartic and therapeutic value in Eco's book, Eco unlike Bakhtin, has no belief in the final liberating effect of carnival.[2] Nor is laughter in Eco's book situated in the body. Laughter is a sign appearing in texts, interplaying with a myriad of other signs. These signs are all ultimately meaningless in the sense that none of them points to a principle of absolute truth or has any foundation in an ultimate reality.

Laughter in the body as seen in Bakhtin versus laughter in the mind as found in Eco describes the modern crossroads of laughter and religion. Both roads have religious references, seriously so in Bakhtin, while Eco's book is a flirtation with the Medieval religious universe of signs. When these authors made connections between religion and laughter, they not only strengthened a secular belief in the liberating effects of laughter, they also encouraged religious belief in the same conviction. Thereby, both works support a tendency in contemporary religion to incorporate laughter in some way or another.

When laughter is incorporated into a religious universe, it can be in the form of a theological treatise where laughter is safely confined within the universe of the text. But laughter can also appear outside texts, in real life, calling forth sanctions from Church authorities as well as criticism from secular institutions, as we shall see below. We will also see how the attempt to establish a connection between laughter and the body is prominent in modern religious thinking, a connection not without problems.

CHRIST AS CLOWN

A remythologization of laughter thrives in secular intellectual circles in the latter part of the twentieth century. And laughter has also turned more seriously religious. The Feast of Fools has been launched as a Christian utopia, and even Jesus is nowadays seen as having a great sense of humour. The reintroduction of laughter in Western Christianity has meant the end of several centuries during which laughter was banned from religious life. When laughter was again heard in the Church, it had not sprung spontaneously from religious soil. Its seeds came from outside the churches, from elements of fantasy and creativity prevalent in the culture of the 1960s. Laughter took root because it met what was conceived of as a lack within Christian faith; the religion with the glad tidings could not be too gloomy. The growth of modern religious laughter is in no way like Medieval Catholicism, in which laughter and the comic flourished as integral parts of Church life. This new laughter is dependent on the general cultural value now ascribed to laughter, and on its combinations with religion in secular culture.

Three themes make up the late twentieth-century alliance between Christianity and laughter:

the cosmic ideal: the playful god.
the soteriological ideal: Jesus as clown;
the anthropological ideal: the laughing Christian.

They are interconnected and have appeared several times in recent decades. These themes have developed (as they had to develop), in the dialogue with the canonical Christian texts and texts written by the Church Fathers and the theologians of the Middle Ages. In this way this new Christian laughter appears, as the old did, at the point of intersection between texts, but its impulses come from outside institutional religion.

In contemporary Christianity, the idea of a laughing Christ is more promising than that of a laughing god. A laughing god has only been sporadically touched upon, for example by the theologian Hugo Rahner (Rahner 1965). Rahner took *homo ludens* as his point of departure when he introduced *Deus ludens*, 'the playful god'.

The term *homo ludens* was used earlier as a title of a book by the Dutch specialist on the Middle Ages, Johan Huizinga. In this book Huizinga created a religious anchoring for the playful side of life and argued for an identity between play and ritual, and, with recourse to Plato, for the idea that the sacred can be included in the category of play. Huizinga's book became a modern classic, and contributed to the launching of the playing human being as an ideal of modernity. Like Bakhtin's work, it got an exuberant reception by the American counterculture in the 1960s, when its title was used as a slogan during student revolts.

Rahner connects the modern concept of *homo ludens* with an ancient concept of god. In his thinking, the image of a playful god is anchored in the tradition of Divine Wisdom (Rahner 1965: 5–9). This tradition originally developed in the intertestamental period, and in the Book of Proverbs, we are told that Wisdom rejoiced, or played (*ludere*) before the face of God since the beginning of time (8: 27–31). When Rahner appealed to a god who laughs, he wisely referred to this hypostatized entity of Wisdom, in this case a substitute for God. This was a reasonable approach, taking into consideration that the Old Testament references to a laughing god had such prominent derisive and mocking connotations and reflected a view of laughter and the divine which fits poorly with the modern view (cf. chapter 1).

Jesus was an even more likely source of joyful laughter than God the Father, even if Christianity had been burdened by the persistent tradition that the saviour never laughed. In 1969, the theologian Harvey Cox wrote a book entitled, *The Feast of Fools*. Cox saw secularization as an irreversible historical process, leading to the liberation of society and culture from religious guardianship and control (Cox 1965). According to Cox, this process of profound liberation had roots in Biblical religion and was a natural consequence of this religion. Cox wanted to talk politically about God and to transcend the theological dilemma of immanence/transcendence. When Cox, in *The Feast of Fools*, reinvented Jesus as a harlequin and a clown, while praising rituals of feast, play and fantasy, he was dependent on ideas expressed by Huizinga in *Homo Ludens* and by Bakhtin in *Rabelais and his World*. Cox shared his interest in a comic or laughing Christ with other contemporary theologians of the 1960s and later (Cormier 1977, Hyers 1981, 1987, Patrides 1983, Samra 1986, Schwarz 1971, Trueblood 1964, Vos 1966, Kuschel 1994).

When Jesus is presented as a comic hero, the arguments usually run as follows: through his message Jesus turned the world on its head, talking against the rulers of this world. Like a clown, he was debased, but never conquered. The comedy of Jesus is seen as an expression of joy without limits, a liberating perspective on life and a new religious ideal. Jesus generates joy and laughter in the hearts of believers. Central to this conception is the idea that the gospels do not relate a tragedy. Taking into consideration that the life of Jesus did not end with suffering and death, but with resurrection, the gospels can be considered closer to comedy than to tragedy. This alternative perspective approaches the text from a non-traditional point of view. It is dependent on contemporary secular conceptions of the clown and on the old ideal of Fools for Christ's sake (saints in the Russian Orthodox Church whose holiness depended on their having violated social norms and faked madness), giving new meaning to the humanity of Christ and to the revolutionary dimension of his teachings (Cox 1969: 139–40).

Some theologians have gone further and argue that Jesus was genuinely funny. In their view, several aspects of the teachings of Jesus are incomprehensible if they are taken seriously. They only become clear when they are taken humorously (Trueblood 1964). Perhaps the audience was expected to laugh when they heard Jesus say that it was 'easier for a camel to go through the eye of a needle than for someone who is rich to enter the kingdom of God' (Mark 10: 25). But such a thesis is problematic. Even if it can be argued that explicit use of humour in the New Testament does exist, as it does in Rabbinical writings from the same period, when it was not uncommon for a good teacher to spice his words with irony, this kind of humour (and irony) was intended to be taken seriously. It would have been exploited for pedagogical purposes in polemic, parables and paradoxes (Jonsson 1965). If the audience burst out laughing when they heard about the rich man and the camel, that laughter was instructive. The primary purpose with that sort of story was not to make the audience laugh, but to teach them.

In any case, it is difficult to make a theology of laughter resting on the concept of a 'witty' Jesus. A far more convincing Christian theology of laughter takes as its point of departure an alternative perspective on Christianity as a comic gospel aimed at liberation and unlimited joy (Kuschel 1994: 65–93). The laughing Jesus is a theological concept and does not pretend to be a true historical picture. The vision of Jesus as a comical hero fits hand in glove with the counterculture of the 1960s and the secularized theology which followed that era. But above all, it opened the door for the laughing Christian.

THE LAUGHING CHRISTIAN

The ideal of the laughing Christian varies. Hugo Rahner, for instance, uses as his starting point the Greek *eutrapelia*, wit.[3] Those who practice *eutrapelia* represent the middle ground between the two extremes of excess in merry-making (*bomolochia*) and boorishness (*agroikia*):

> Just because so many 'bomolochoi' are active in our world and slip into the obscenities of ancient Attic comedy, we Christians are not obliged to become 'agroiki', but must try to realize the Christian ideal of the serious-serene human being at play in his fine versatility, in eutrapelia, in that serene abandonment to the seriousness of God.
>
> (Rahner 1965: 104–5)

For Rahner, the source of *eutrapelia* is the incongruity between the inadequacy of all created things and the perfection of things divine. Rahner leans heavily on Thomas Aquinas, while Aquinas was dependent on Aristotle (Rahner 1965: 98–105). The ideal laughter is, according to Rahner, moderate, controlled and never eruptive. It is clearly in accordance with the Christian tradition, which as we have seen, preferred spiritual over bodily laughter. Rahner's concept of laughter was theologically correct and in line with that of his predecessors.

Though Harvey Cox referred to Rahner, he was more radical than Rahner and did not limit himself with earlier theology. His concept of laughter was directly influenced by his own age, not least by Bakhtin. Cox was not so afraid of the 'lower' forms of humour as Rahner appeared to be. On the contrary, Cox claimed that something of the Dionysiac 'is returning in force to contemporary Christianity' (Cox 1969: 55), and he combined the values of festival and fantasy with social criticism, and argued for reclaiming the body. When Cox eloquently sings the praises of the 'natural body', he went further than Rahner, who only made the moderate point that play is an activity which engages both soul and body (Rahner 1965: 6–8):

> To reclaim the body with all its earthy exquisiteness in worship is a hopeful sign only if it means we are ready to put away our deodorants and prickliness and welcome the body's smell and feel back into our ascetic cultural consciousness. Only when that happens will we know that our civilization has left behind the gnostics and their wan successors and has moved to a period when once again we can talk about the redemption of the body without embarrassment.
>
> (Cox 1969: 55)

Cox made a clever observation and developed this idea into a social critique: a Church which affirms the body may also support a less repressive social order. As he saw it, the Church was at odds with the ruling assumptions of modernity, therefore it was weak and even ridiculous. Perhaps, Cox says, the conception of Christ as clown and harlequin was fitting for the Church in the 1960s, as it was for the early Church (Cox 1969: 141). In Cox's thinking, Christ as a clown, the Church in the post-Christian era, the reinstallation of the body, and the laughing Christian are all linked.

Cox's laughing Christian is a radical recreation of religious man in a secularized world. According to Cox, it is only possible to make sense of traditional religion by assuming a playful attitude toward it. This playful attitude is built on a confrontation between critical reason and traditional belief, in which reason and belief are brushed aside in a comical liberating perspective. As seen in most contemporary research on humour and in accordance with the

113

incongruity theories of humour, humans have an innate ability to hold two or more contradictory ideas at the same time. From the tension between these ideas, humour and a new perspective may arise. In the clash between reason and belief, and between the present world and the world to come, a dual perspective arises which can be exploited as a matrix for laughter and humour.

As for the kinship between play and religion, Cox focuses especially on prayer and claims that play and prayer are both acts of disciplined fantasy. He argues that prayer can be sung and danced, as well as spoken, and again turns the focus from the mind and the head of the believer to his/her whole body. For Cox, the significance of laughter is profound: it is a fundamental characteristic of human beings and necessary for the maintenance of their human worth. Laughter is hope's last weapon, 'and where laughter and hope have disappeared man has ceased to be man' (Cox 1969: 157).

Rahner and Cox differ in their conceptions of laughter, but they both argue that it is theologically and existentially desirable for Christians to pursue a witty or comic attitude toward life. This view has recently been developed in more explicit therapeutic directions. In Christian charismatic movements, a belief in the therapeutic effects of salvific laughter is combined with the old myth of the devil's fear of laughter. Consequently, there are divine services in which people are asked to laugh and laugh and thus force the devil away, though this practice is not without its opponents. Some warn against it because it means giving too much attention to the devil, others argue that in laughing at the devil, we underestimate his evil powers.

In the middle of the 1980s a book by American theologian Cal Samra, *The Joyful Christ: The Healing Power of Humor*, spoke of the second coming of Christ and the defeat of the devil when all evil and all barriers between people will be blown away by divine laughter:

> Christ came to us bringing peace, love, joy, laughter and healing. And when he returns again, he will lead his disciples in a chorus of laughter, because, as the old saying goes, the Devil can't stand the sound of laughter.
>
> (Samra 1986: 11)

Samra's aim is to establish the healing power of laughter and its value in the true Christian life. He supports his case with Church history on the one hand, and medical theories on the other – the modern and popular physio-chemical theory that laughter stimulates the brain to manufacture natural pain-relieving substances, the endorphins, and the older physiological theory that a good laugh gives exercise to the internal organs and helps circulation. Samra describes Jesus as the Great Physician and as the greatest psychiatrist of all times (Samra 1986: 37). The idea of Jesus the clown is combined with the idea of Jesus the healer. Samra argues that just as so many health professionals from different disciplines are now using humour in their practice, Jesus, the healer of healers, must also have used humour to calm the ill, allay their fear and cheer mourners.

In Samra's book, cosmological laughter has come down to earth and become incarnate. Samra suggests several practices for incorporating laughter in religion and church. One of them is to create clown ministers and introduce clown services. Samra initiated the 'Fellowship of Merry Christians', a grass-roots ecumenical movement with some hundred members in which ministers dress as clowns in their services and serve the communion. Modern 'fools for Christ' visit hospitals and mental institutions to deliver hugs and jokes (Samra 1986: 39–51). Samra's own alter ego is 'Brother Zorba', an allusion to the famous novel by Nikos Kasantzakis where laughter and merriment are presented as true tokens of religiosity. The organization also sells pictures of a laughing Christ. Through its newsletter, *The Joyful Noiseletter*, which according to its own advertising is the Christian world's most reprinted and quoted newsletter, the 'Fellowship of Merry Christians' reaches a multitude of American churches, furnishing them with 'hilarious holy humor' and comic cartoons for their parish magazines. The newsletter gives the congregations 'a strong dose of good cheer, good humor, clean fun, and healing laughter'.[4] What is the purpose of this humour and what is being joked about?

In the *Noiseletter*,[5] God's presence is evoked through the column 'The Lord's laughter'. The column consists of jokes quoted from newspapers, magazines, books and people.[6] In each edition, the column is followed by the quotation of the first half of Psalm 2: 4, 'The One whose throne is in heaven sits laughing' (the second part of the verse, 'The Lord is mocking them' is notably not mentioned). The *Noiseletter* has a cosmological aim. It involves the idea of two worlds, the present and the one to come. When kept together, these two worlds can function as a matrix for a comic perspective on life, as argued by Rahner and Cox. The Easter miracle, the resurrection of Christ and the victory over death should fill Christians with

115

permanent joy. Therefore Samra's fellowship also designates itself and its mission as the 'House of Laughter', after Lazarus' home in Bethany which got this name because of the tradition that Lazarus laughed heartily for years after Jesus raised him from the dead. As expressed on the back page: 'Our modest aim is to recapture the spirit of joy, humor, unity and healing power of the early Christians. We try to be merry more than twice a year.'

This cosmological aim is also more directly expressed in the content of the newsletter. An average '*Noiseletter*', containing about five to eight cartoons, ten to twenty jokes, funny stories and *bon mots*, and four to five smaller articles is consciously intended to make people more open to the gospels. The *Noiseletter* is meant to 'tickle the congregation to life':

> Many pastors tell us that just one timely cartoon or a funny anecdote or a joyful Scriptural message from our award-winning newsletter puts their congregation in a good mood – and more open to the Gospel and to worship – from the very start of a service. Leaders of prayer groups and support groups report the same phenomenon.
>
> (from 'An invitation to join our "House of Laughter"')

In short, the *Noiseletter* is a weapon against churchly boredom. This is an interesting point. In the Middle Ages the opposition between the world to come and the present world was reflected as an opposition between the evangelical ideal of poverty and the reality of an all-powerful and worldly Church. One strand of Medieval religious humour had a strong social and moral motivation. Another Medieval matrix for humour was the opposition between the body, the corruptible and material part of humans, versus the soul, their spiritual and divine part. The American denominations of today appear to have different contexts for their humour. One is the contrast between this world and the one to come. Dull services versus revolutionary salvific message is another contemporary matrix for Christian joking.[7] In contrast to modern religious laughter, Medieval laughter poured forth from the strong brew at the centre of Medieval Christianity, when the powerful Church was contrasted with the true Christians, the mighty with the powerless, soul with body.

The jokes of the *Noiseletter* often take Church life as their point of departure, as in the cartoon where a wife gives her husband, the minister, friendly advice when he leaves for the church: 'Don't call anyone sinner until *after* the collection' (9, 1, 1994: 3) or in another cartoon where a priest asks his wife after having read his sermon aloud to her, 'So for the most part, that'll be my sermon. What do you think the reaction to it will be?' The wife is sound asleep (9, 2, 1994: 3). These cartoons do not question belief as such. Children appear frequently as where a little girl asks, 'Was St. Patrick married to Cleopatrick?' (9, 3, 1994: 3) – or where a little girl has gone to bed, and left lots of space beside her in the bed, saying to her mom, 'I hafta leave plenty of room for my guardian angel and those big wings' (9, 3, 1994: 5), or the girl who says to two smaller boys, 'Know what? Washington, Lincoln, and Jesus were all born on holidays' (9, 2, 1994: 1).

The *naïveté* and honesty of the children seem to represent the values of the world to come. Their roles and sayings confirm the words of the gospels that the kingdom of God belongs to small children (Matthew 19: 13–15; Mark, 10: 13–16; Luke 18: 15–17).[8] The *Noiseletter* has a large percentage of children in its cartoons and comic strips. They reflect how the modern Christian life aims at the nuclear family, but more important, the presence of children guarantees that these jokes are 'clean'.

The ideals of *Deus ludens*, Jesus as clown, and the laughing Christian do not represent a break with common Christian values and do not lead to critical questions or to sacrilege. In other words, they represent 'clean' laughter within traditional faith. Their goal is to enhance spiritual values; the laughter they evoke is used instrumentally to make speech less boring and to encourage believers, but not to create change and havoc.

JOKES OF CRITICISM AND DOUBT

Clean jokes may only tickle the ribs. Dangerous jokes, on the other hand, may strike to the heart while being very funny. Outside Christian institutions, a field of *critical laughter* exists, stretching from mild criticism of religious themes and institutions in cartoons, to more daring jokes found in contemporary culture, and further to texts and moving images which have been labelled blasphemous. The first category, the syndicated newspaper cartoons, offers cultural reflection and criticism of religion, but not in a way that seriously undermines the values of religion or questions religion as such. These cartoons are generally acceptable to society. Their general aim is to reinforce norms, not to question them (Alston and Platt 1968, Lindsey and Heeren 1992).

Other jokes do not hesitate from eliciting a laugh at the cost of religion. Their targets are those elements of Christian faith which are difficult and ambivalent. The goal of these jokes is to challenge traditional Christian faith by means of impertinent questions and deconstructive tactics. Such challenges to Christian tradition are found, for instance, in jokes about sex and sexuality connected with the divine figures.

The mythology of Christianity stresses a trinity which is indisputably male: God, Christ and the Holy Ghost. The sex of this triad is often not explicitly focused upon, but it functions as a powerful source of legitimation in the religious universe. This domination of the maleness of the Trinity is reflected, for instance, in the strong opposition against female priests and against homosexuality. Because the symbolic significance of sex and sexuality is so obvious, and models for procreation and family relations are so essential in the Christian universe, its mythology is especially vulnerable to sexual jokes, as we saw much earlier in the sardonic remark of Piron about the cuckold, the whore and the bastard. A contemporary example of joking about sex and God is the following story:

> God has the blues. St. Peter suggests a trip to earth to pick up a nice Greek girl, possibly in the old swan suit. God says, 'No. As long as I stuck to those Greek girls it was all right. But once I made the mistake of knocking up a Jewish girl, two thousand years ago, and I'll be damned if they're not still talking about it.'
> (Legman 1978: 885)

While this sort of joking at God's expense may be for the most part accepted, it has not been widely accepted to make Jesus an object of jokes (Walter 1990). It could be, as has been suggested, because the character of Jesus has no traits that serve as natural targets for jokes (Legman 1978: 887). More likely, the relative lack of malicious joking about Jesus in mainstream culture reflects the position and value of Jesus in the Christian universe (cf. chapter 7, n. 4).

In our secular world, doubt shadows religion. Such radical doubt is a source of jokes and mockery. For a contemporary example: a little boy, lost in the wood, prays to God on his knees for help.

> As he kneels praying, a bird flies over him and drops a load of shit into his outstretched palm. The little boy examines it and turns his eyes back to heaven. 'Oh please, Lord,' he begs, 'don't hand me that shit. I really and truly am LOST!'
> (Legman 1978: 889)

The theologian Gerhard Schwarz uses another such joke about doubt in the opening to his discussion of the death and resurrection of Christ. Although Schwarz does his best to take the sting out of the joke, its point goes to the heart of Christian belief and Christian doubt.

One Jesuit has got permission to make excavations in Jerusalem. Eventually he finds the grave of Jesus, unfortunately including his bones. The Pater General is sent for. Together with different specialists, he travels to the place to make an inspection. Again they open the grave, and make sure that there is no mistake. No mistake has been possible. They stand staring at the bones. After a long while one of the Biblical specialists is overheard, mumbling to himself, 'So, after all, he has really lived!' (Schwarz 1971).

In a time when even priests come forward saying that they do not believe in the dogmas of the Church, it is not surprising to find radical doubt also expressed in theological treatises. Clearly, this joke is built on a contrast between a realistic and a religious interpretation of events, a mechanism we also saw at work in the Roman empire examples of critical laughter aimed at religion. Schwarz's joke refers not only to doubt about the bodily resurrection of Jesus, but to the more fundamental doubt about Jesus having ever lived at all. In addition, this joke includes connotations of that type of Biblical criticism which does not leave any fraction of traditional belief safe for scientific exploration, and which has forced theologians in the last century to give up stronghold after stronghold of their creed.

ROLLING IN THE AISLES

So far, we have seen how laughter is used religiously to bring out the real message of the glad tidings, or to reveal critical differences between secular and religious claims of truth.

Another type of laughter at work in the modern religious world is the laughter that appears in some charismatic movements. This laughter, even if it is meant to be therapeutic, works in a rather violent and unpredictable way, and could therefore be described as chaotic. As we have already seen in connection with the ancient Greek gods, chaotic laughter is laughter working as a channel between the human and the divine, but in an unstructured way. The most well-known recent example of this type of laughter is found in a charismatic movement which originated in Canada with the

Toronto airport branch of the Vineyard Christian fellowship. In the mid-1990s, people are flocking from different parts of the world to take part in what they conceive of as a charismatic revival. At the same time, the phenomenon has spread to other churches in Canada, as well as to the USA and Europe.[9] The connection between uncontrolled laughter and other uncontrolled bodily movements is striking in this movement.

In the church in Toronto, the worshippers sing rock hymns and many wail and faint during the service, falling to the floor. Some giggle, others shake with laughter and roll about in the aisles. Animal noises such as barking, howling and cackling are heard. In England, the centre for the movement has been Holy Trinity Brompton church where the same sort of phenomenon can be witnessed: there is clapping and dancing and dozens of people bursting into laughter or tears, trembling and falling to the floor. Two-hour-long queues for the Sunday evening service at this church have been reported.

Who or what is the source of this phenomenon? Is the turbulence created by the Holy Spirit, by Satan, or do other forces stand behind it? The participants themselves see the laughing turbulence as a strong intervention of God in the world; they believe they are witnessing the Holy Spirit at work. Uncontrolled fits of laughter are explained as possession by the Holy Spirit. John Arnott, a leader in the movement, characterizes it as 'holy laughter' (*Boston Globe*, 29 April 1996). The interpretation of outsiders has not been so benevolent. For instance, when John Arnott started a tour in England, the question was asked in the *Guardian*: 'Has a humble community in urban Canada felt the touch of the Lord, or has it made a home for the devil?' (31 January 1996). This question is the same one Church authorities have been asking: are these fits of laughter during services in reality the work of the devil? Other newspaper headlines have suggested other explanations, just as critical: 'Spread of hysteria fad worries Church' (*The Times*, 18 June 1994), which is in accordance with how the phenomenon was explained in the preface to the Church of England Yearbook in 1994, where it was characterized as 'an expression of mass hysteria'. Psychologists generally write the phenomenon off as a form of group ecstasy, without especially explaining the laughing. But laughter in this movement is significant. It appears like a sort of key symbol, defining the movement for those who adhere to it as well as for its critics.

Why does laughter enter into this type of movement at all?

Generally speaking, charismatic movements are fuelled by the need for religious experience, and for the believers to feel the personal intervention of God. As for laughter, its presence might partly be explained by the generally positive light in which laughter is viewed today. As we have seen, to introduce laughter into religion is a trend in modern theology as well as in the life of Christians: Christians should be merry and show it. But more than this, the uncontrolled movements and outbursts during the services incorporate a religious practice in which laughter is a vehicle for religious experience not yet fully controlled or understood. The opposition and discussions which the movement has provoked reveal that this type of religious practice is at best regarded as ambivalent, at worst as threatening. Such reactions further reflect that it is still possible for laughter to appear as a channel to an unknown land of which one does not know who is in charge – God, the devil or irrational forces of the human psyche. The eruptivity of this laughter, and its opposition to orderliness and reason, clearly connote a body which behaves without rational control. When people fall to the floor, roll about in the aisles, no longer speak rationally but express themselves through inarticulated outbursts passing for laughter, the body is really returning to religion in force. The believers are confronted with the need to interpret bodies rather than texts, and to furnish these bodies and their laughter with an acceptable Christian interpretative framework.

This type of bodily practice is problematic in Christianity, a religion based on words and texts. When laughter is part of a bodily language allowing a direct channel into that which is not defined by Christian dogma, it is regarded with uneasiness. If mainstream Christianity is to include laughter, it must be defined and contained. It cannot be allowed to appear as an uncensored expression of the irrationality and eruptivity of bodily life.

As we have seen, the connection between laughter and the body in contemporary religious thinking is ambivalent. As we turn from Zorba, the Christian priest, to Zorba, the Buddha, from Christianity to New Religious Movements, we move from ambivalent attempts to write the body into religion again to a not so ambivalent attempt to get rid of it.

7

RELIGION OF JOKES
Flirtation with the East

There is fun in heaven. God can play practical jokes upon Himself, draw chairs away from His own posteriors, set His own turbans on fire, and steal His own petticoats when He bathes. By sacrificing good taste, this worship achieved what Christianity has shirked: the inclusion of merriment.

(A Passage to India, Forster 1949: 301)

During the twentieth century, the East has inspired new thinking, symbols and practices in the West. The West has been engulfed in an Asian renaissance in which the recreated East stands forth as a source of wisdom and spirituality, in contrast to the materialism and technology of the West (Sloterdijk 1989). India is viewed as the land of spiritual metaphysics, while China and Japan are seen as developing a more practical wisdom. The West has created the East in its own inverted image: because religion in the West has been a serious business whose figures were famous for never having smiled, it is to be expected that the wisdom of the East would come laughing (Hyers 1974).

BUDDHISM COMES LAUGHING

And so it has: deep spirituality is detected in the enigmatic smiles of the Buddhas and the belly laugh of the Zen monks. The Buddhas and monks have always smiled and laughed. What is new is the significance Western interpretations give to these old religious expressions. The laughter of the holy men of the East is seen as a token of their self-realization and liberation. We want to share the joke to receive part of their supposed superhuman knowledge.

However, the degree to which Indian religions are depicted in the

West today as promoting jokes and laughter represents a transformation of these religions to fit a Western audience. Strictly speaking, ancient Indian Buddhism was not a religion which approved of unrestrained laughter. On the contrary, it spoke against it. Did Buddha laugh? A scholastic discussion similar to the one conducted in Christianity regarding Christ took place in India nearly two thousand years ago. Philosophers discerned six types of laughter. For those in authority and of high caste, only the two 'highest' forms were appropriate, the faint smile (*sita*) or the smile which slightly revealed the tips of the teeth (*hasita*). The loud laughter that brought tears to the eyes and the uproarious laughter that shook the body back and forth and made it collapse were signs of low origin and an unruly character (Aung 1929: 22–4). It probably goes without saying that Buddha only partook in the barely perceptible smile of *sita*.

This restricted smile of Buddha is seen in classical Indian statues where Buddha is depicted in *samadhi*, a state free from thoughts and feelings. Closed to the world of the senses, his eyes are shut and an introverted smile lingers on his closed lips, barely perceptible. This smile has been likened to the *risus sardonicus*, the smile of the dead, because Buddha is dead to the world (Fingesten 1970). It could as well be likened to the early smile of the new-born baby because the new Buddha is born through enlightenment. Neither the *risus sardonicus* nor the smile of the new-born are caused by external stimuli; both are appropriate for the enlightened one. Perhaps these forms of smile, that of the new-born and that of the dead, meet in the figure of Buddha. In any case, the restricted smile is in accordance with the question, 'How can anyone laugh who knows of old age, disease, and death?' (*Buddhacarita*, 4, 59) and 'How can there be mirth or laughter when the world is on fire?' (*Dhammapada*, 146). Like the smiles of the early Christian virgins of which the Church Fathers were so fond, Buddha's smile is a denial of laughter. It reveals his self-sufficiency and his closure toward the external world.

This serious tradition was challenged by the Chinese and Japanese forms of Zen Buddhism. In Zen, the masters and the monks are described and depicted with thick bellies and with open mouths roaring loadly with laughter (Moore 1977: 176–7). Theravada, an early and still vigorous form of Buddhism, and Zen represent two types of conduct toward the world, and two types of smiling and laughter, thus suggesting the breadth of Buddhism. In an apocryphal story dear to Zen, one of Buddha's disciples revealed his enlightenment through a wordless smile. The smile was transmitted by a succession of twenty-eight Indian patriarchs before Bodhidharma took it to China, and the smile gave way to thundering laughter. In the Chinese Buddhist tradition of Zen, salvation is built on life in this world, promoted by spontaneity, unconventional questions and jokes.[1] The experience of enlightenment is often described as triggering laughter (Morreall 1989).

Zen Buddhism has been one of the most important religious influences on the Western counterculture (which has generally been a seedbed for new religious impulses). In some branches of Zen, humour is used to break through the tangle of concepts and reach direct experience. There is 'often a kind of comic midwifery in the Socratic sense of a technique for precipitating (or provoking) an inner realization of the truth' (Hyers 1989: 270, also Hyers 1974). The goal of a fruitful opening up of the body is present in Zen in the use of laughter and joking.

The smiles and laughter of Buddhism are also reflected in another branch of Buddhism which is well known in the West, namely Tibetan Buddhism as personified by Dalai Lama, the God King, the living Buddha. One typical example is that when Dalai Lama visited Madame Tussaud's in 1993 to see his wax image, the difference between the real Dalai Lama and the model was only one thing, according to the newspapers; one of them could not stop laughing (*Daily Mail*, 2 November 1993: 19). This example illustrates how laughter symbolizes a new type of religious ideal in today's Western world.

This joking attitude, reflecting buoyancy and *joie de vivre*, blends with elements from Hinduism, Taoism and Sufism – religions and philosophies which are influential in the West in the late modern period. These movements have in common that they stress the power of mind. Common for several of them – and typical for the Hinduistic philosophy of Advaita Vedanta, especially in its Neo Hindu style – is also how they see an ultimate unity behind the manifold world. Different ways lead to this Truth, but none of them is identical with the Truth, which can only be reached through individual effort of meditation and concentration. These movements lay stress on the universal self and not on a personal god. Because these movements presuppose an incongruity between what is and what seems to be, they also establish a matrix which could be used as a universal starting point for laughter and jokes.

In many New Religious Movements, humans and their latent

universal self are given enormous importance. Connected with the focus on self is also the idolization of the charismatic, exalted master. In several cases, this master tends to be the focus of the movement and a model to be worshipped, and thus this master appears as vastly more important than any individual self. The background of this kind of exaltation may be Indian, but its reception in the West was probably made easier by the model of Christ. As a former member of one New Religious Movement, that of Bhagwan Sri Rajneesh, phrases it: 'You are encouraged to believe that you too, are God, but it's a theoretical belief merely, as it is allowed no expression which conflicts with the official precedents: Bhagwan is the Goddest' (Belfrage 1981: 193).

Modernity's idolizing of the charismatic, exalted master had an early archetypal moment when Vivekananda appeared at the World Parliament of Religions in Chicago in 1893 praising the holy man Ramakrishna. Then the educated West was reintroduced to the veneration of the living god-man. Of course this new holy man had a sense of humour:

> Unlike the Jesus figure presented by the writers of the Synoptic Gospels, when reading . . . of the behaviour of Ramakrishna one is struck by his wonderful sense of humor, skill at telling jokes and funny stories, and delight of his laughter. His keen sense of humor is enjoyed by his followers who find his laughter contagious.
>
> (Olson 1990: 69)

Such is the stuff of which modern saints are made: they laugh, Jesus did not. (At least, except for the Gnostics, he did not laugh before the second part of the twentieth century.) Jokes and laughter are natural expressions in this new world of religions; all means by which humans can expand their consciousness and achieve their true potential are legitimate. One New Religious Movement that systematically included techniques of laughter and developed a jocular and playful attitude was that of Bhagwan Sri Rajneesh. He is an extreme example of how Indian religion has been reinvented and transformed in a Western context.

THE JOKING GURU

For Bhagwan Sri Rajneesh (1931–90), later called Osho, laughter and jokes were a trademark. Bhagwan Sri Rajneesh did not behave like the holy fools of the Orthodox Church who were often frowned upon by contemporaries and were the butt of jokes. Bhagwan was a master of the joke and in control of laughter.

Born in a Jain family, Bhagwan established a community in 1974 in Poona, India, after having quit his career as a university teacher of philosophy. He attracted many Westerners, and in 1981 eventually moved his community to the state of Oregon, USA. In 1985 he was deported from the United States, accused of immigration violations, and spent the last part of his life in the ashram in Poona.

Bhagwan Sri Rajneesh was a charismatic personality, greatly loved by his adherents, and experienced as god by some of them. Ma Satya Bharti described her living with him in Poona as, 'God lives in the house next door to me, thirty feet away' (Bharti 1981: 3). Central to Bhagwan's teaching was freedom from all religious beliefs, from the idea of God and from dogmas in general: 'I want to take God away from your life, so that you can feel yourself for the first time independent, free, not as a created puppet but as an eternal source of life. Only then you can rejoice' (Rajneesh 1989: 80).

Similar to many of the contemporary New Religious Movements, Bhagwan's communities were centred around the individual. Bhagwan believed that to achieve self-realization, both body and mind had to be worked upon to develop a new consciousness. Thus Bhagwan pursued goals typical of modernity's focus on self and on individual identity. Its techniques were – if inventive and varied – not fundamentally different from many of those therapies which flourish in the West. Seen in a broader comparative perspective, the stress on laughter and on a joking attitude was not primarily a feature which made Bhagawan's groups stand out in relation to other religions and religious groups. On the contrary, Bhagwan's emphasis on laughter must rather be seen as an expression of the late modern attitude in which concepts and values are relativized, and absolute truth is nowhere to be found. Consequently, the laughter of Bhagwan's religious movement was not constructed on the margins of modernity, but at its very centre.

The essence of Bhagwan's teaching was the fundamental wholeness of the individual's body and soul. All the same, one can distinguish the development of the body and the development of consciousness as two distinctive strategies in the Bhagwan movement. The practices of Bhagwan Sri Rajneesh and his followers illustrate a concept of the body common to late modernity and which is generally ambiguous. The body stands in permanent danger of invasion from the outside, from physical but invisible forces that will penetrate and destroy it. A goal is to preserve the body's life, health and youthful appearance. The care given to Bhagwan's body reflects that goal.

Bhagwan's body was considered important because it was the abode of his divine consciousness. It was a gateway to divinity and was treated as an icon: when, in Rajneeshpuram in Oregon, he drove by in one of his many polished Rolls Royces, hailed by his adherents, we recall the vehicles and beasts used to carry the godhead in the mythology of India and elsewhere. We are also reminded of the old Indian image where the soul resides in the body as a charioteer in the chariot. Analogously, the car with Bhagwan inside could be read as an image of body and consciousness. Bhagwan, 'the blessed one', was the ideal man, and therefore his was the model body. This body was taken excellent care of and was meticulously groomed. Bhagwan was clad in long robes, usually white, made with loving care by some of his disciples. He had matching hats and a beautiful beard. According to Ma Satya Bharti's description, he 'looks exactly as God would, if God were to choose to look like anything' (Bharti 1981: 7).

One of his former adherents, Sally Belfrage, emphasized how Bhagwan's body was cared for, but her conclusion is different from Ma Satya Bharti's:

> He seems so healthy: I have never seen anyone look healthier. Why all the anxiety about the imminent failure of this body? Another trick? If he's really rotten to the core they've done a remarkable polishing job. That's it: He looks polished, buffed, like very expensive fingernails.
>
> (Belfrage 1981: 140–1)

Sally Belfrage sneers at Bhagwan's baldness: 'He poses for new photographs wearing all kind of funny hats (How could God be bald?)' (Belfrage 1981: 193).[2]

Parallel with the care for the body of the master, grounded in adoration and worship, ran anxiety for the body's safety. Bhagwan's body was extremely vulnerable. It was open to physical attacks from the outside and had to be continually guarded against assaults. In order to ward off physical attacks, Bhagwan had a bodyguard with him on stage when he was lecturing. But dangers operated on the microlevel as well. Bhagwan's health was said to be fragile. The commune feared invasion of his divine body by everything from odours to germs and poison. Those who wanted to attend his meetings had to pass two guards who put their noses into the visitors' hair to make sure they did not reek of body odours or of perfumes, a precarious balance: people often had to wash their hair several times to be sure they passed the 'sniff-test'. Those who had an illness were told to keep away and if they did not, they were turned back at the gates.

Because Bhagwan's ideal was that man should be sensuous and spiritual at the same time, both enjoying the body and being a great consciousness, sex was practised rather freely in the early years and sexual tantric techniques were explored. But in 1984, the fear of AIDS emerged. Bhagwan then introduced new and strict procedures for safe sex; he recommended either celibacy or fidelity, and the adherents were told to use condoms and gloves. And even if Bhagwan still postulated that life was 'a feast and not a fast' and taught 'rejoicing not renouncing', the attitude to sex changed. He had described sex as a force which went to the root of being because it penetrated directly with no resort to abstractions (Rajneesh 1980: 376). Now sex was also drawn into the context of a body besieged by physical but invisible dangers, and became part of a clinical procedure rather than an expression of carefree play.

At the same time as the body was groomed and protected, it had to be actively worked upon by means of different techniques for self-realization, techniques that were dynamic, violent, noisy and direct, and sometimes stripped the body naked. While Bhagwan was believed to have reached a level of higher consciousness, his adherents were continually working towards it. The reflexive restructuring of body and self, so dear to high modernity, had virtually its Mecca in Poona, which was a laboratory for religious techniques, and which still offers a wide range of development courses. Those who lived in Poona and Oregon in the days of Bhagwan Sri Rajneesh were offered a combination of theory and practice: daily lectures by Bhagwan (now from tape) and a rich variety of courses in such things as encounter, primal therapy, gestalt, bio-energetics, Rolfing, Tantra, Yoga and meditation. From the courses in Poona the self-realization techniques spilled over into manuals and guidebooks, competing with the general flood of therapeutic books of all sorts in the modern world: the care for the body and the self has become a serious matter indeed (Thompson and Heelas 1986: 10). The dynamic techniques were apparently applied to the body, but in reality they were aimed at consciousness. The body was, when all was said and done, only of limited interest.

A KEY SYMBOL

In Bhagwan's movement, a resistance to ideas and dogmas was accompanied by a wish to experience reality directly.[3] Laughter encompassed basic values of Bhagwan's teaching, especially in that it provided a channel to a direct experience of reality.

Bhagwan's delight in jokes was persistent. (At the same time his critics tended to see Bhagwan himself as a joke: 'his delivery is like a pantomime snake "You musssst", he is inclined to hiss, "have a senssssss of humourssss"' (*Guardian*, 28 May 1982, in Mullan 1983: 9).) In Poona, Bhagwan lectured every morning and jokes were an integral part of the lectures. The jokes did not necessarily have a profound spiritual depth, any kind of joke would do – and did: many of them were rude and childish but the audience still exploded with laughter. Bhagwan explained his ability to always have the right joke to illuminate any kind of point in a simple way: the joke had priority; the spiritual point was put around the joke afterwards (Bharti 1981: 9). The jokes were taken from joke books or sent to him by his adherents. They were usually reflections of the values of the Western world, as in the ironical point of this fashionable feminist joke: on the question of why Bhagwan referred to God as He not She, he answered that since God is indisputably feminine, the least one can do is call God He (Belfrage 1981: 196).

Although Bhagwan was the master of the joke, the custom of telling jokes was used by his adherents as well. For instance in Rajneeshpuram in Oregon, joke-telling was mandatory at every council meeting (Mullan 1983: 133). Jokes are also part of the literature of the movement, apart from in Bhagwan's books. The first number of the British edition of *The Rajneesh Times* started with three jokes on its front page, pertaining respectively to Jesus, to the Rajneeshee themselves and to politicians.[4] These jokes were probably deliberately chosen, reflecting central concerns of the movement in Britain at that time: how to characterize itself in relation to traditional religion, how to establish a self-image and how to describe its relationship to the surrounding world.

Laughter was cultivated not only in the context of jokes. Laughing Meditation was also taught and encouraged. Consisting of five minutes of pure laughter with the purpose of losing oneself, it was to take place in the morning after waking up and stretching. If it was difficult to laugh spontaneously, a drink of lukewarm water with salt was recommended to clean the passage and make an opening up.

Laughter would make the one who laughed see the absurdity of life, change the nature of the day and activate the body. Laughing Meditation was an echo of the much longer Dynamic Meditation, which in a similar way completely activated the body until it exploded with shouting, jumping, singing and laughing. In Dynamic Meditation active phases were contrasted by a phase where the body was frozen and silent (Rajneesh 1983: 29–30). The contrast between the extremes of silence on the one hand and action and loud noise including laughter on the other, is an example of the bringing together of extremes typical for Bhagwan's followers. His followers were urged to 'melt in the silence of the ten thousand buddhas', 'dissolve in the laughter and celebration of the ten thousand zorbas', and 'go wild in the Carnival of Life' (*Osho Times International*, 1 December, 1992).

For Bhagwan Sri Rajneesh, to be a *sannyasin*, a holy man, clearly meant to be in a festive mood. Bhagwan saw laughter as a primary signal of the holy state and it was therefore encouraged and cultivated. People smiled and laughed a lot in Bhagwan's ashram, and he had special joking relationships with several of his disciples:

> Japanese Geeta had a shrill and startling laugh which used to make Osho laugh whenever He heard her. He would stop speaking and they would simply be laughing together, apparently at nothing, while the rest of us would catch the infectious laughter and eventually everyone would be laughing. He said that laughter is the greatest spiritual phenomenon.
>
> (Shunyo 1991: 124)

Instances of unquenchable laughter are recorded by his disciples, even at solemn occasions such as initiation into the community: Ma Satya Bharti laughed herself to pieces when she was initiated to be a *sannyasin* and received the *mala*. She began to laugh and laugh uncontrollably. She continued to laugh for hours, as she also did on a later occasion: 'The laughter went on and on. I remember hearing the sound of it coming out of me, and wondering where it had been hiding for all those years' (Bharti 1981: 23).

Bhagwan was not satisfied with only making people laugh. For him the experience of laughter was exploited as a symbol in a mytho-poeic discourse on cosmology. That cosmology embraced the individual and the world. Ma Satya Bharti expresses this cosmological thinking on laughter most expressively:

Life is unendingly funny. Do you see it; do you feel it? I suffer, therefore I am. I laugh, therefore I am not. When 'you' are not, when the ego dies, only laughter is. Existence is one big belly-laugh, a beautiful joke. The birds are laughing, the trees are laughing, the stars are laughing, the Buddhas, the Christs and the Bhagwans are laughing. Only we sit, locked inside our conditioning, with unsmiling faces.

(Bharti 1981: 24)

In Ma Satya Bharti's texts, commenting upon Bhagwan's teaching, laughter becomes the very expression of the dynamic unity of existence: developing images with roots respectively in Zen and Hinduism, the face of laughter is described as the original face of man before his mother and father were born, and the whole universe is said to throb with the sound of laughter (Bharti 1981: 163). The power of laughter can for a moment stop the individual from thinking rationally and thus be an awakening:

It is possible, when you have a hearty laugh, mind stops – because mind cannot laugh. It is structured seriously; its function is to be serious, miserable, sick. The moment you laugh – it does not come from your mind, it comes from the beyond, from your very inner spirit.

(Rajneesh, 1989: 98)

But laughter can also be a power which reaches out from the individual and changes the world completely: 'Just think for a moment on the whole world laughing, dancing, singing – just for one hour' (Rajneesh 1989: 81). When Bhagwan was expelled from the USA, 3,000 'rajneeshee' assembled in Milan under a huge helium balloon with the words, 'If only the world will laugh for 24 hours . . . Bhagwan Shree Rajneesh' (Mullan 1983: 136). And finally, in 1992, the death of the master was commemorated with a world wide laugh-in where 10,000 adherents in Poona laughed together with 20,000 others from other communities across the world (*India Today*, January 1931: 81–97). The ring of laughter across the world was to create joy and peace, a special variant of belief in the cosmological power of psychic vibrations shared by many of the New Religious Movements.

Because laughter was placed at the heart of his religion, as its very essence, Bhagwan also used laughter to explain the division between his religiosity and the other religions: 'According to me, all the religions have missed one of the dimensions of great importance; that is the direction of sense of humour. They have made the whole world serious' (Rajneesh 1989: 98). Bhagwan's heroes were especially Buddha, Bodhidharma and Jesus, as well as Gurdjieff and Krishnamurti from modern times. However, he contrasted himself and them because of their attitude to laughter and humour; he claimed that several of the old masters had never laughed: 'Jesus would not laugh, Buddha would not laugh, Lao Tzu is not heard to have ever laughed. They were serious people, and they were doing serious work' (Rajneesh 1989: 97). However, Bhagwan is not consistent on the question of whether Jesus and Lao Tzu ever laughed. Sometimes he said they never did, other times that they did, as when he claimed that Lao Tsu was born laughing and could laugh a belly laughter. As for Jesus, even if the Christians and the Hindus say that he never laughed, that would, according to Bhagwan, be impossible, because then he would not have known anything: 'Jesus must be a belly-laugh, otherwise it is not possible' (Rajneesh 1975: 225). He also commented on Zarathustra, who according to tradition, was born laughing, and frequently returned to the delightful stories about Mulla Nasreddin, the clown of Arabic tradition. It is, of course, no coincidence that several of Bhagwan's books are comments on mystic wisdom traditions, such as Zen Buddhism, Taoism, Sufism and Gnosticism: clowns and mystics have always gone well together, probably because they share a knowledge of the relativity of all ideologies; laughter and mysticism goes hand in hand (Gilhus 1991b: 272–3).

Bhagwan divided laughter into three categories: (1) belly laughter which is an immediate reaction to a joke, not taking the detour of explanation; (2) laughter from the head, in which understanding goes before laughing; (3) laughter which imitates others' laughter. It goes without saying that this typology is a hierarchy of values.

ABSOLUTE SELF/RELATIVE WORLD

In his struggle to establish the oneness of being, Bhagwan was backed by centuries of Indian intellectual elites working to satisfy their unquenchable thirst for the absolute. But all the same, his quest was modern and its reception typical of the late twentieth-century Western world. The situations he faced were ones that the earlier holy men of the Indian religious tradition, such as Shankara and Caitaniya, could never have dreamt of: not only did Bhagwan's followers tackle rapid and radical changes in the community's life, but after Oregon, when their master was flying around the globe, trying to find a place to land and stay, they also had to cope with countries which had him deported or denied him entry. That was an acute lesson in the relativity of being and the vulnerability of the individual.

In the modern world the development of the self is in focus, but surrounded by doubts and risks (Giddens 1991). With Bhagwan's stress on human potential and his focus on the development of the individual, the surrounding world became a backdrop and the body a gateway. The plethora of jokes helped to keep it like that. The more real the self became, the more unreal the world, the less worthy of true commitment (Carter 1990: x). For his adherents Bhagwan's habit of saying one thing one day, and something completely different the next, revealed the relativity of truth and their master's superior outlook (Bharti 1981: 68–9). His critics saw it differently:

> Rather than be caught out by any criticism, he [Bhagwan] calls his behaviour deliberate, a joke or a test or a trick. How can he lose? Simply by allowing himself to be called God, he inspires the double-edged perception that, while God would never do such a thing, who but God would have the gall?
>
> (Belfrage 1981: 193)

Bhagwan did not invent the practice of telling jokes in a religious context. On the contrary, it must rather be seen as typical for the modern religious leader – not least among Christian charismatic groups – to excel in joke-telling. Generally speaking, the Western world is brimming with jokes, oral and written; there is no escape from them. What do all these jokes tell us about our world? Like the slave whispering in the ear of Caesar to make him remember in the midst of his glory that he was mortal, jokes continually mumble about the relativity of this world.

For Bhagwan, like many of his predecessors in the history of religions, laughter was an opening up of the body. That does not tell us anything new. Nor is it new to think of the body as a gateway to the soul. What is new is that the body has now lost its lasting significance and been deprived of its future: eternal salvation or damnation is no longer waiting for it. Bhagwan's epitaph sums up this position and reflects one of late modernity's dreams, the belief in reincarnation: 'Never born. Never died. Only visited this planet

Earth between December 11, 1931 and January 19, 1990.' While humans are visiting this earth, they are tied to a body. Curiously, this body has become ambiguous in a new way, and frequently appears more like an enemy than a friend; not only because of its susceptibility to disease and vulnerability to physical attack, but also because bodily reality blurs the true reality of the self. In short, the body is blocked up and in acute need of being opened (Thompson and Heelas 1986: chapter 3). Therefore it has to undergo treatment: an early strategy of Bhagwan was to open it up by means of sex. But after the threat from AIDS, this procedure became dubious. Laughter was a safer option, causing the same opening, but giving the body only a minor shock, without risking death. Fortified with laughter, Bhagwan appeared not so much like a midwife as like a surgeon, violently cutting his ways into the depths of human beings. Figuratively speaking, laughter became a wound in the body. When Bhagwan praised laughter because it joined all three dimensions of a human's being – body, mind and being – he spoke from a relative and temporary point of view. In the context of a belief in the transmigration of souls, the praised unity between body and soul was a transitory phenomenon, laughter only a heuristic device. Compared with human's real self, the body turned out to be insignificant.

In Bhagwan's teaching, laughter wormed itself into the consciousness of the believers, poking fun at their perishable bodies and cutting them loose from these transient unreliable material vehicles. To that purpose, explanations of laughter and the systematization of laughter – in short, a discourse on laughter – were cultivated in Bhagwan's ashram. In a broader perspective, this discourse can be seen as part of the reflexivity of modernity, and a strategy applied to tackle universal doubt. In a way, this doubt is typical for modernity and a constituting factor in Bhagwan's thinking.

This look at Bhagwan Sri Rajneesh and his movement – with its extreme reflections of modern themes such as the ambivalent conception of the body, the focusing on self, radical doubt and the stress on laughter as a liberating force – has brought us to the end of our journey. Our examination has taken us from laughing gods, weeping virgins, and serious monks to the company of an utterly modern joking guru. It is time to reach a conclusion.

CONCLUSION

Humans build bridges to the divine world through their narratives and rituals of laughter. All the same, laughter is an ambiguous way to go, not without its dangers. And while human beings may laugh at gods and disturb the sacred world, gods may laugh human beings to pieces and destroy them. Laughter transcends language and is frequently used as a characteristic of the divine: the Mesopotamian Anu, the Israelite Jahweh, the Greek Dionysos and the Gnostic Christ were all laughing gods, and so is the late modern Jesus. Through their laughter gods show their power and transcendence, their superiority over human beings as well as their closeness to them.

We started this analysis with presenting two opposing phenomenological fields in which laughter was invested with both life-giving and destructive values. In the pre-Christian period, erotic, creative, magic and comic laughter opposed the laughter of trickery, the tragic laughter and the chaotic laughter. In the Christian period, laughter's regenerative potential was expressed in spiritual laughter and embodied laughter, while laughter's destructive qualities found their outlet in rationalized and critical laughter. Therapeutic laughter is characteristic for the modern period, but regenerative laughter may also appear as utopian laughter and as chaotic. Derisive laughter, on the other hand, may take the form of blasphemy.

Laughter can be harmless, as when it flirts with that which everybody knows, that which is easily put into words and that which everyone dares to say. But when laughter touches that which is not yet said or allowed to be said, perhaps not even thought, then laughter is no longer only a polite accompaniment to speech, but rather a dangerous power. In spite of all attempts to control it, laughter may open up experiential channels to enigmatic realms. In all periods, we have witnessed how laughter draws sap from that which is not expressed in speech and from desires and feelings which perhaps have no words. Normative religion usually portions out the unknown in digestible bits and keeps the irrational within bounds. The laughter of the Dionysiac cult was tamed when the god appeared in the Athenian theatre, thereby exploiting the hidden forces without succumbing to them. Dionysos and other Greek gods are specimens of an extreme category: laughter appearing spontaneously and eruptively. The opposite extreme, in which laughter is utterly controlled, is exemplified by the virgins and monks of the early Church. Most forms of laughter, however, appear in between these extremes. In charismatic movements, for instance, a ritualization and routinization of laughter will appear gradually, reducing the spontaneous element – the participants will be *expected* to laugh. However, it is not always possible to obtain anticipated laughter at charismatic meetings, which shows that the phenomenon is not completely predictable. The means of keeping laughter as an eruptive phenomenon and controlling it have varied through the centuries.

In the earliest texts, the symbolism of laughter was clearly rooted in bodily symbols. Derisive laughter appeared in narratives of biting and castration where teeth and swords were parallels to laughter. Regenerative laughter was found in myths and rituals where it interacted with a symbolic world of female bodies, birth, sexuality and erotic forms. Anchored in bodily symbolism, both derisive and regenerative laughter had emotional depth, irrational grounding and multivalence.

Regenerative laughter appeared as creative, magic, comic and erotic. Perhaps most interesting is how the erotic and the ludicrous were intertwined in myths and rituals, especially connected with women and the cult of goddesses. It seems as if erotic laughter partook in ritual and cultural processes where desire and emotions were allowed to fertilize the ritual experience with less restraint. Myths of creation, magic rituals and comedies exploited regenerative laughter in instrumental ways and generated forms of laughter that were probably more controlled than erotic laughter. The derisive laughter appeared in an atmosphere of cunning, skill and trickery among humans as well as among the gods. A sharpening of derisive laughter made it tragic and utterly destructive. Its strongest irrational grounding was established when derisive laughter appeared as chaotic and outside human control.

In the Christian era, laughter was drawn into the context of the individual body. Compared to the earlier period, a great change in the symbolic and ritual use of laughter happened when laughter was condemned because it was associated with bodily life, and especially with eroticism. How erotic life was exorcized from religious laughter and replaced with spirituality is one of the great dramatic changes in the history of religious laughter in the West. This change may be connected with how religious interest moved from the relationship between human beings and the world to human beings and their spiritual life. In Christianity, the body appeared as the stage for the drama of individual salvation, thus playing the double role of being a vehicle for salvation and an alluring trap. This paradoxical situation was a starting point for laughter's versatile career within Christianity. Laughter was restricted by the early Church, made into mythology with a vengeance by the Gnostics, but blossomed in the late Medieval Church. The early Church as well as the Gnostics spiritualized laughter; they made it refer either to piety or to *gnosis*. In the Middle Ages, different forms of bodily laughter came to the fore, as a carnivalesque celebration of the material body or as a devoted worshipping of the flesh and blood of the saviour. In both these phases of Christianity, the human body was the dominant interpretative context of laughter.

Christian theologians inherited from Greek philosophy both a dislike of laughter's eruptivity and a belief in its usefulness, and their ambivalent attitude has accompanied the Christian history of laughter from the Church Fathers to contemporary theologians. This attitude is consistent with Christianity's focus on rational speech and with its ambiguous attitude toward the human body. However, laughter has obviously had a certain power to generate meaning even when it is restricted. For instance, the ideal lives of monks and virgins of the early Church reflect how laughter was constructed and displayed precisely by its being forbidden. All the same, it is reasonable to say that regenerative laughter had a marginal existence in the early Church. Derisive laughter, however, seems to have flourished, partaking in cultural processes in the Roman empire which led to the creation of Christianity and to the eradication of other religions.

Until the modern period, religious laughter has undoubtedly been grounded in a symbolic world, where the emotional and the bodily life of human beings was strongly present, furnishing laughter with a certain kind of depth. In modernity, however, there seems to have been a change. Laughter's grounding in bodily and emotional life is no longer so prominent, and today laughter is recast more as a cognitive phenomenon. An endless string of jokes is the preferred vehicle of modern religious laughter. This shift has probably contributed to laughter nowadays tending to appear more as a surface phenomenon.

The last hundred years reflect a dramatic change in laughter's religious credibility and use. Across religions, laughter is now both a permitted and encouraged religious expression. Laughter has partly moved from its previous context of the individual body and has risen again as a phenomenon of the mind. But at the same time as laughter is conceived of as a phenomenon of the mind, it is given symbolic value in relation to the body and treated as a bodily sign. This duality can be seen in secular variants of religion, in contemporary Christianity, as well as in New Religious Movements. It reflects that the position of the body in relation to the self is ambiguous and open to various interpretations.

A primary aim of modern religious laughter is liberation, its *modus vivendi* is therapeutic, but its results are not necessarily either therapeutic or liberating. Therapeutic laughter is part of the modern ideal of keeping the individual happy and healthy, and thus is considered a positive force which should be cultivated. The rehabilitative qualities of laughter are not so much an expression of genuine merriment as an expression of the general rationalization of modern society. Laughter has become an object of calculation and control, to be measured and manipulated by psychology, the social sciences and the entertainment industry. At the same time, laughter is paradoxically seen as a means of working against rationalization. The same sciences which so successfully made laughter a subject for their knowledge are now busily showing how laughter gives access to joy, play, fulfilment, wisdom and liberation. In the modern world of religions, then, laughter is controlled and used with certain defined purposes – be it to make churchly boredom more easy to bear or as a strategy of tackling radical doubt by neutralizing it. As a liberating force, laughter is utopian.

Since saviours and believers generally are dependent on each other, laughter's new status has led to the invention of a laughing Jesus and to the introduction of joking gurus on the modern scene. How the modern religious space of laughter is created and what its mythological references and aims are vary across religions. A fit of laughter can be a manifestation of the Holy Spirit if one is a Christian, or an experience of unity with the divine if one is a follower of an Eastern guru. In other words, laughter may still appear as a channel to the divine, and its religious role is not exhausted by therapy and jokes. In spite of present-day laughter partaking in processes working for rationalization, laughter may also work against these processes, as in the Toronto Vineyard movement. Here laughter appears as a vehicle for a religious experience which is eruptive, out of control and can be explained in different ways.

Laughter is culturally constructed, and so are its types and the phenomenological fields with which we have been working. In reality, these types and fields overlap. One example is how an experience of laughter as an opening up of the human body fertilizes the imagery evolving from the laughter symbol, both when laughter is life-giving and when it is destructive: laughter gives birth and laughter gobbles up. Another example is how the strange rhythm of chaotic laughter pulsates between the regenerative and the destructive.

To abandon oneself to laughter means the temporary unmaking of one's traditional self and the letting loose of a violence that sweeps the outlived away, makes the body blaze and makes the world vibrate with life. But in the dark depths of laughter, life-giving and destructive values meet and intermingle, and ultimately these depths are impenetrable for human thought.

NOTES

INTRODUCTION

1 The body has been a focus of many different interpretations this century. To mention some examples, the philosopher Maurice Merleau-Ponty wrote a phenomenological work, *Phenomenology of Perception*, originally published in French in 1945. The French philosopher Michel Foucault has made a 'genealogical' approach to the body, as seen in *Discipline and Punish: The Birth of the Prison* (1977). The British social anthropologist Mary Douglas is famous for her structural and anthropological approach to the body, for instance in *Natural Symbols* (1970).

2 This theory was first formulated by Aristotle. Other prominent representatives of the theory include Hobbes and Henri Bergson.

3 Aristotle also touched on the incongruity theory. In recent years theories of incongruity have been elaborated in different fields, e.g., anthropology, linguistics and semiotics, making incongruity theories the most elaborated area of humour research with a near consensus that incongruities are necessary ingredients in all jokes. Theoreticians who have discussed incongruities in humour include Arthur Koestler, Gregory Bateson, William F. Fry, Mary Douglas, G. B. Milner, Walter Nash and Victor Raskin.

4 The first protagonist for this type of theory was Herbert Spencer (1820-1903); its greatest advocate was Sigmund Freud. His book about jokes is an investigation of laughter and the meanings of jokes. For an application of his general theories of the unconscious to this special area of human display, see Freud 1983.

5 The first international congress of humour was held in Cardiff, Wales, in 1976 (Chapman and Foot 1977). Annual congresses of humour are now held, and the first number of the periodical *Humor: International Journal of Humor Research* appeared in 1988.

6 The construction of the body in late antiquity and in Christian thought has been a focus of growing interest in recent years (Brown 1989, Foucault 1990, Stroumsa 1990).

1 THE ANCIENT NEAR EAST: LAUGHTER OF DERISION AND LAUGHTER OF REGENERATION

1   The myth flourished in Mesopotamia, but the oldest version of it comes from Tell-el-Amarna in Egypt. Egypt and Babylon were the great powers of the Near East in the second millennium. They had close political connections and scribes in the pharaoh's administration knew Akkadian. The myth is also recorded on tablets from Assur, of the late second millennium BC. The text is actually found in four fragments, B from Amarna, while A, C and D were from the library of Assurbanipal. (See Bing 1984, de Liagre Böhl 1959, Kienast 1973, Müller 1983, Roux 1961, Sauren 1988.) For the text, see Dalley 1989.

2   In D 4 Anu laughed over what Ea had done, in B 66 over Adapa.

3   Anu's laughter can be explained as benevolent (but this is not a likely explanation): the offer of eternal life could have been a test, which Adapa passed when he did not eat and drink and thereby showed that he knew man's place to be on earth. It could even have been that what was the Water and Bread of Life for the god of heaven would have been poison for human beings, because their place was on earth and not in heaven. In that case, because Adapa had not let himself be tempted, Anu laughed a laughter which was approving and fatherly. The flaw with this and similar explanations is that they do not leave room for any conflict in the myth.

4   The Hurrians were a people, who in the second millennium BC, dominated northern Mesopotamia, northern Syria and part of Asia Minor. The myth is found in the so-called 'Song of Kumarbi'.

5   The myth occurs in 'The contendings of Horus and Seth', 4, 3, Papyrus Chester Beatty I (Lichtheim 1976: 214–23).

6   The motif of divine striptease and laughter as a remedy against a situation stuck in gloom is found in several cultures. In Japan it is the mighty sun-goddess Ama-terasu who is teased into laughing. The myth describes a struggle between Ama-terasu and her violent brother, Susa-no-wo, who manifests himself in the wind and the tempest. Susa-no-wo is a destructive force of nature, while Ama-terasu is a giver of life. (For a recent discussion of the myth, see Miller 1984.) In the Japanese myth, as well as in the Egyptian myth, indecent female exposure and laughter is the turning point between death and life. The mytheme also exists in Greece, connected with Demeter and Baubo, and will be discussed in the next chapter.

7   The connection to tears was probably inspired by a pun. The Egyptian word for 'mankind' is *remet, remyt* is the word for 'tears' (Gugliemi: 1980: 907–8).

8   Several articles have been written about laughter and humour in the Bible (see, e.g., Lang 1962, Patrides 1983, Radday and Brenner 1990, Reines 1972).

9   The primary terms for 'laugh, play' are *ṣḥq* and *śḥq*. The oldest term was probably *śḥq*. There may have existed a sense of differentiation between the two; *ṣḥq* has sexual connotations in some of its occurrences as verb forms. Both primary roots have a potential lexical neutrality, while in

actual usage in most of their occurrences they express contempt and ridicule. The same holds true for derived terms. The semantic field of these terms is discussed by Alethaya Brenner (Brenner 1990).

10 The texts discovered at Ras Shamra made the picture of the religious history of Palestine more complex and caused the Hebrews to lose their monopoly on interpretation of their relationship with the Canaanites: in these texts, Syrian Canaanites who lived in the second millennium BC made themselves heard. The six tablets from Ras Shamra, inscribed about 1380–60 BC, were copies of older texts, preceded by an oral transmission of the myths. Thus they are divided from the Old Testament by a great span of time, but suggest that it is a late monotheistic interpretation of a Canaanite world of ideas (see Loretz 1990).

11 The divine councils in Canaanite, Phoenician and early Hebrew sources are similar to each other. These assemblies, consisting of both major and minor gods, helped the chief god but had no power apart from him (Mullen 1986).

12 The laughter of the Ras Shamra texts and the laughter of the Old Testament are in marked contrast when it comes to erotic laughter. In the Ras Shamra texts, laughter appears in a context of fertility and eroticism opposed to death and weeping, as well as in an aggressive context. His wife, Anat, laughs when she tells Baal that a house has been built for him (*Baal*, 4, v, 25); Kotharu-and-Khasisu laughs when Baal says that a window shall be opened in the palace and a rift in the clouds, probably to let the rain flow (*ibid.*, 4, vii, 21); El laughs when he sees in a dream that Baal lives and that heaven will let it rain oil and the wadis will flow with honey (*ibid.*, 6, iii, 1ff.). Laughter is life-giving too when the goddesses ask El to make them pregnant (*KTU*, 1, xii, 12). Derisive laughter is found when Anat is killing her enemies, probably the life-threatening forces (*ibid*, 1, ii, 25). Anat was a goddess of war; battle, violence, lamentation, mourning, love and fecundity (Kapelrud 1987). Her laughter is evil when she plans to kill Aqhat (*Aqhat*, 1, vi and 2, i, 22). Texts consulted are found in Moor 1987.

13 Even if words for laughter are not used to describe religious joy in the Old Testament, that does not mean that uncomplicated joy and happiness did not exist abundantly in Israel as reflected, e.g., in the Psalms: 'Sing aloud to God our strength; shout for joy to the God of Jacob' (Psalm 81: 1), or when king David and the people danced and sang before God (2 Samuel 6: 5, 21), and Wisdom rejoiced before the face of the Lord (Proverbs 8: 30–1). But joy is seldom described as laughter (an exception is in Psalm 126: 2).

14 In 1 Samuel 2: 1, Isaiah 57: 4, Psalms 35: 21, 81: 11. Also She'ol, the Underworld, is metaphorically described as having an open mouth (in order to swallow). This metaphor may be a reminiscence of a conception of death as a laughing monster, Isaiah 5: 14; Habakkuk 2: 5. See Brenner 1990: 56–7.

2 GREECE: WHEN LAUGHTER TOUCHES THE UNTHOUGHT

1   In Greek *gelao* has the meanings 'laugh', 'smile' and 'laugh at'. There are several derived terms (Liddell and Scott 1968). *Geloion*, 'the ludicrous', covers both the comic and jokes (Süss 1969). The vocabulary for laughter is extensive and rich. According to Stephen Halliwell at least 'some sixty word-groups are directly pertinent' (Halliwell 1991).

2   The god of laughter in Greece is usually Dionysos. But according to Plutarch, legislator Lycurgus dedicated a little statue of Laughter in Sparta, (*Lycurgus*, 24, 5). What this Lacedaemonian worship implies is not known. Gelos is never identified with Dionysos (Milanezi 1992).

3   The *komos* was a merry revel on the festival days of Dionysos. Comedies and satyr plays were common property and from the sixth century BC supported by the city in annual festivals. Both sprang out of religion. The symposion was often held in temples at festivals, but was not in itself a religious ritual.

4   Stephen Halliwell draws a distinction between playful and consequential laughter. This contrast overlaps with a distinction between *geloia* and *spoudaia*, without being identical with it. Playful laughter is indicated by *paizein* and related terms (Halliwell 1991: 281).

5   According to Dillon, 'in approximately 70 of the 80 extant examples from tragedy, laughter may be characterized as malevolent in extreme, and is equally prevalent in Aeschylus, Sophocles and Euripides' (Dillon 1991: 345).

6   The story of Prometheus describes how the division of the different parts of the slaughtered animal was made. This was an important subject in Greece, because the majority of rituals had sacrifice at their centre. The sacrifice divided gods from men and men from beasts, it made communication between gods and men possible and the consumption of meat a lawful and pious act (Vernant 1991). That the gods had to be content with the inedible parts of the animal – thighbone, pelvis and tail – was an inexhaustible source of fun for the comedy authors (Burkert 1985: 57).

7   Hesiod pretends that Zeus saw through Prometheus' cunning, but chose the poorest portion so as to be able to punish men for their deceit – a characteristic combination of myth and piety on the part of Hesiod (West 1966: 321).

8   L. M. West characterized this laughter as 'the cackle of triumph' (158), similar to *Iliad*, II, 318, 21 (West 1978: 408).

9   Cf. Arnobius, *Adversus Nationes*, 5, 25. For the relation between Clement's version and Arnobius' version see Marcovich 1988, where the one is reduced to the other. A different view and an interpretation of the passage in Arnobius is given by Olender (Olender 1990: 88ff.)

10 Demeter nursed the son of the queen of Eleusis, Demophon, and made a deal with Hades so that her daughter was released from the Underworld and could stay with her mother two-thirds of the year. Afterwards she 'sent forth fruits from the fertile fields' (471) and founded her rites at Eleusis.

11 Sources are a scholion on Lucian's 'Dialogue of the courtesans',

Aristophanes' comedy, *Thesmophoriazusai* and some minor notices. According to the scholion on Lucian, Thesmophoria was celebrated in accordance with the old myth of Demeter and Persephone.

12 The importance of this feast is illustrated by Aristophanes writing a comedy about it. The feast was celebrated at Athens in the autumn month Pyanopsion, the fourth month of the year, from the eleventh to the thirteenth. For recent discussions of Thesmophoria, see Dahl 1976, Detienne 1989, Versnel 1993, Winkler 1990, Zeitlin 1982.

13 Cf. the title of Winkler's article, 'The laughter of the oppressed: Demeter and the Gardens of Adonis', in Winkler 1990: 188–209.

14 The oldest of the three genres may have been the satyr play, a mixture of comedy and tragedy. This is rather peculiar, because the Greeks taught us to separate the tragic from the comic. The form and the themes of the satyr plays are similar to those of the tragedies, and they were staged in connection with them at the Great Dionysia. Like the comedies they are full of coarse joking, but it is not so indecent, and like the comedies they have happy endings. (For a general introduction, see Seaford 1984.)

15 Their closest relatives were silenoi and centaurs. The centaurs have the body of a horse, but are men from the breast; satyrs and silenoi have the ears and the tail of the horse, in the beginning also its legs and hoofs.

16 The success of *Frogs* was so great that it was staged more than once, which was unusual (Dover 1972). Comedies were originally staged at Lenaia at the end of January, later also at the greater festival, Dionysia, at the end of March.

17 For recent interpretations of the play, see Foley 1985. Foley reads the play in connection with a cognitive universe reflected both in sacrifice and theatre. See also Seaford 1996, Versnel 1990 and Vernant 1990b.

18 See Foley 1985. With the words of Albert Henrichs (Henrichs 1993: 19): 'When provoked by mortals, he confronts them directly and stares them down – the frontal face and the irritating smile are visual hallmarks of Dionysus' self-revelation in art and literature.' In his recent commentary on the play, Seaford remarks that the god is laughing, not just smiling (Seaford 1996: 186).

19 The German theologican and historian of religions, Rudolf Otto (1917), has characterized the power in religion as *tremendum et fascinans*; it makes human beings tremble and fear at the same time as it fascinates and attracts. In Dionysos this force has the added characteristic of *risans*; laughter is intermingled with fear and fascination and generates those emotions in its objects.

3 ROME: CRITIC OF LAUGHTER AND CRITICAL LAUGHTER

1 Aristotle, *Poetics*, 1449a. This commentary is poignant. Distortion was indeed a characteristic of many of the comic forms in Greece, not only of the theatrical masks, but of the comic actors in general who were entertainers with a hanging belly and artificial phallus. The satyrs and the figure of Hephaistos are also characterized by distorted bodies.

2 Cicero, *De Oratore*, II, 54, 219–20.
3 According to P. G. Welsh this festival is probably an invention made by Apuleius and not to be connected with Gelos in Sparta (Welsh 1994: 247).
4 This was a widespread point of view, see also Juvenal, *Satire*, XIII, 34–48.
5 *The Assembly of the Gods* was written at a time when the emperors tried to reform the qualifications required for membership in the Aeropagus. It has been claimed that the dialogue is primarily aimed at contemporary issues in Athens: 'the mythological material is more the vehicle than the target of the satire' (cf. Branham 1989: 164). The situation in Athens is probably one layer of Lucian's work, but it seems unlikely that the mythological material is only the backdrop. By his sketch Lucian strikes precisely at the contemporary religious situation, and that was most likely also one of his aims. (See the discussion in Oliver 1980, Branham 1989: 164–6.)
6 In his exposure of contemporary religion, there is one area that Lucian does not touch, the cult of the emperor. Dead emperors, living emperors and members of their families were worshipped as gods. Lucian's lack of interest in this cult could be because he saw it more as political ceremony than a religious phenomenon in its own right. However, others did not take this cult quite seriously. The philosopher Seneca outrageously mocked the divinity of the emperor Claudius (*Apocolocyntosis*). One of the 'gods-to-be', Vespasian, uttered a famous line as he was dying, 'My goodness, I think I am turning into a god', revealing a half-joking attitude toward the religious content of the phenomenon (Suetonius, *Vespasian*, 23).
7 Even if Christianity was the cult which grew fastest, especially in the eastern part of the empire, scarcely more than one out of fifty had become Christians by the third century AD. Among their contemporaries their beliefs were not very well known (Benkor 1980).
8 This passage had frequently been commented upon by Greco-Roman authors. Cf. Ovid, *The Art of Love* 2, 561–92; Lucian, *Dialogues of the Gods*, 17 (*Hermes and Apollo*).

4 EARLY CHRISTIANITY: LAUGHTER BETWEEN BODY AND SPIRIT

1 Jesus is never pictured laughing in the New Testament. However, the laughter of Jesus is sometimes found in apocryphal texts, for instance in The Gospel of Pseudo-Thomas, where the child Jesus laughs rather maliciously (Hennecke and Schneemelcher 1959: 290ff., Rudhardt 1992: 405, n. 68). Even if laughter has no prominent place in the New Testament, it has been the subject of investigation (Jonsson 1965). Jesus was met with mocking and disbelieving laughter when he was about to raise the daughter of Jairus from the dead (Matthew 9: 18–19, 23–5, Luke 8: 53, Mark 5: 40).
2 Cf. also James 4: 9: 'Lament and mourn and weep. Let your laughter be turned into mourning and your joy into dejection.' According to

Paul, 'Entirely out of place is obscene, silly, and vulgar talk' (Ephesians 5: 4).

3 Ecclesiastes is one of the most recent and most personal expressions of the Israelitic wisdom tradition. In general God's laughter seems to have stuck in the throat of later generations of Jews. Obviously, it no longer fit in with God's exalted majesty. When the rabbis singled out divine laughter for special comment, it was probably because they found it strange. Luke's use of the term 'laughter' is in opposition to contemporary Judaism which describes salvation as joy, but not as laughter. An exception is Rabbi Simon ben Yohai who said that when God delivers Israel the mouths of the saved would be full of laughter *(Berakhot,* 31 a, in Reines 1972).

4 The same punishment was given for spitting in the assembly, getting off to sleep or being so poorly dressed that one's nakedness was seen.

5 Athanasius' description is in this case taken nearly verbatim from Porphyry's description of Pythagoras (Bremmer 1992: 208).

6 The virgin must be seen in parallel to the monk: in monastic orders talking was restricted; some enjoined silence. Here the dialogue between men and the world had come to an end and was replaced by the dialogue between man and god (Bergmann 1985, Fuchs 1986).

7 In Greek rhetoric and later in the Roman authors there existed a mixed style where comic elements were used to spice the serious. *Ioca seriis miscere,* to mix the jocular and the serious, was an accepted literary style (Curtius 1953: 417).

8 Early commentaries on the Gnostic laughter were made by John Dart (1975) and Günter Bröker (1979). The following books are useful introductions to Gnostic religion: Jonas 1963; Rudolph 1978; Filoramo 1990. For the Nag Hammadi texts, see Robinson 1988.

9 The hypothesis of a Pachomian origin of the Nag Hammadi library has many supporters and opponents. For a recent discussion, see Khosroyev 1995.

10 About Seth, the problem of the Sethians and the Sethian texts, see Klijn 1977, Wisse 1980, Turner 1986.

11 But there are examples of the Valentinians also using laughter mythologically. According to one of their myths, the material world originated from the passion of a mythological being called Achamot. Spirit, however, was born from her laughter. This laughter is connected with her relaxing and with her remembering the lost spiritual light and is opposed to her fear and grief (Irenaeus, *Against the Heresies,* I, 4, 2). In other words, laughter has a creative and slightly positive function in this myth.

12 For the etymology of the name, see Scholem 1974 and Black 1983.

13 The Gnostic world-creator is a complex figure and this type varies in different groups and texts. (See Filoramo 1992: 77ff. and 118, n. 22, which contains references to articles which discuss this fascinating figure.) The Sethian texts describe him most negatively (Gilhus 1984).The Valentinian demiurge on the other hand is just, but ignorant.

14 The Gnostics seem to have had an absorbing interest in the creation myths of Genesis. Jewish scholars had already made erudite comments

upon these myths and new interpretations of them. The Gnostics were thus heirs to a rich tradition which they used to their own purpose.

15 Cf. Karen King: 'The text's use of mockery, wit and ludicrousness show a strong sense of play and a talented penchant for narrative entertainment' (King 1990: 10).

16 The Valentinians had a more positive view of Jesus and a more complex Christology.

17 Christ laughing at the crucifixion is found in one of the other texts from Nag Hammadi (*The Second Treatise of the Great Seth*, CG, VII, 2, 55: 30–56: 19) and also in connection with Basilides (Irenaeus, *Against the Heresies*, I, 24, 4.) In both these cases it is Simon from Cyrene who substitutes for Jesus: 'Jesus himself assumed the form of Simon and, standing by, ridiculed them.' Origen (*Commentaire sur l'Evangile selon Matthieu*, XIII, 9) speaks of Christ laughing with scorn at the ignorance of those who crucified him (Perkins 1980: 180).

5 MEDIEVAL CHRISTIANITY: CARNIVAL, CORPUS CHRISTI AND BODILY LAUGHTER

1 Parallel to the European development, systematic thinking on laughter took place in the context of Islam (Rosenthal 1956, especially 'Appendix on laughter').

2 Hugh of St Victor said that serious things tasted better if spiced with kind mockery. John of Salisbury allowed seemly mirth (*modesta hilaritate*) (*Polycraticus*, I, 8). Hildebert of Le Mans permitted a few jests in the midst of serious work, but advised that they be carried out in a worthy manner (*Libellus de IV Virtutibus Vitae Honestae*, PL 171, 1060 c) (see Rahner 1965).

3 The oldest mention of the feast is at the end of the eleventh century, by the Rector of Theology in Paris, Joannes Belethus. Charles Du Fresne Du Cange says that there are four *tripudia*, religious dance feasts, after Christmas. The feasts belong respectively to the deacons, the priests, the choir-children and the subdeacons. The last feast is called the Feast of Fools. The common dates for its performance in the different churches in France are the Circumcision, the Epiphany or the octave of the Epiphany (du Cange 1954: 481).

4 The name of the feast is usually *festum fatuorum*. The feast is also called *festum follorum*, *festum stultorum*, (the Feast of Fools), *festum subdiaconorum*, (the Feast of the Subdeacons) and *festum baculi* (the Feast of the Rod) (cf. Chambers 1954: 275).

5 Thomas Aquinas voices a similar opinion when he uses the image of a bow. Like man's mind it would break if its tension was never relaxed (*Summa Theologica*, qu. 168, art. 2).

6 In 1199 the Bishop of Paris, Eudes de Sully, wrote a decree against 'the Feast of Fools' (*festum fatuorum*) in Notre Dame (Chambers 1954: 277–8). Like the Theological Faculty 250 years later, he wanted to reform the feast and stop its abuses. The feast was also condemned most sharply by Jean-Charlier de Gerson, Rector of the Theological Faculty of Paris, in 1400.

7　Primarily in the form of *proses et farsurae*, additional chants or interpolations into the text, varying from being harmless to being pointedly improper.

8　'The misogyny of the later Middle Ages is well known ... Male and female were contrasted and asymmetrically valued as intellect/body, active/passive, rational/irrational, reason/emotion, self-control/lust, judgement/mercy, and order/disorder' (Bynum 1986: 257).

9　*Offas pingues*: *offa* is a lump of food or cake made of flour. It has the interesting secondary meaning of 'mass' or 'lump' and even of 'abortion'. With *pinguis*, 'fat', it designates a pudding made of blood.

10　*Incensabitur cum boudino et saucisa*: 'Boudin: mets fait avec un boyau rempli de sang et de graisse de porc' (Littre 1958: 139).

11　The priests were ordained for the *corpus Christi*, the Pauline designation for the Church. From the twelfth century, the *corpus Christi* referred to the Eucharistic body of Christ. This clearly underlined how the body had moved into the centre of religious events and how the cultic role of the priest and the string of identifications between priest, sacrament and Christ had been stressed. At the same time representations of the tortured Christ had become prominent and the believers showed great preoccupation with his sufferings. The Eucharist thus expresses a paradox in twelfth- and thirteenth-century religion: on the one hand the priest was treated as nearly divine because he was the sole person who could administer the Eucharist. On the other hand, the humanity of God in the suffering of Christ was stressed. In this way strong emotive forces were connected with strong ideological interests.

12　The role of the Ass has repeatedly been discussed by scholars, over the last centuries (Backman 1952, Chambers 1954, Greene 1931: 534–49, Villetard 1911). The so-called 'Prose of the Ass' exists in several manuscripts and its use is documented in Bourges, Beauvais and Sens as part of the *Officium* of the day of the feast. A revised version of the text used in the feast is preserved in the *Missels de Fou* from Sens (*c.* 1220) (Dreves 1961: 217–29). This is a text that the subdeacons were allowed to use during the Mass on the Feast of Asses (*asinaria festa*). Neither this hymn nor the general text of the office is offensive. There exist two similar manuscripts from Beauvais. One of them has an *Officium* which is longer than that of Sens and stems approximately from the same time. Beauvais also gives us in addition a description of a procession, representing the Flight into Egypt. In this procession an ass carried a young girl with a child in her arms. Here too, a version of the Prose of the Ass was used (du Cange 1954: 460–1).

13　Thus he is fulfilling the prophecy of Zechariah 9: 9: 'Rejoice, greatly, O daughter Zion! Shout aloud, O daughter Jerusalem! Lo, your king comes to you; triumphant and victorious is he, humble and riding on a donkey, on a colt, the foal of a donkey.'

14　In the canonical gospels the ass does not appear in the nativity scene. In two of the apocryphal gospels, however, the *Gospel of Pseudo-Matthew* and the *Gospel of James* it is found. The *Gospel of Pseudo-Matthew* exercised a great influence on the iconography in the Middle Ages. Here it is said: 'On the third day after the Birth, Mary went into a stable and put the

Child in a manger, and the ox and the ass worshipped it. Here the prophecies of Isaiah and Habakkuk were fulfilled' (Himmer 1980).

15 In Mosburg the 'bishop' is in the sixteenth century also titulated as *asinorum dominus* (Chambers 1954: 319–20).

16 Carnival in the narrowest sense is a designation for the festivities in the half-week before Lent. It designates here festivities characterized by wearing of masks, status-reversals and riotous revelry.

17 The Feast of Corpus Christi was founded in the mid-thirteenth century and celebrated as a universal feast from the early fourteenth century. It was held on the Thursday after Trinity Sunday, a movable feast which fell between 4 June and 6 July (modern calendar).

18 Discussions of the plays and their relation to religion are found, for instance, in the thematic approaches of Kolve (1966) and Prosser (1961), and in the comparative approach of Woolf (1972). In the two recent decades there have been two main approaches to the cycles, either the thematic study of the individual cycle or a comparative analysis of the same episode in all the cycles (see Staines 1991). Richardson and Johnston (1991) explore the relationship between the plays and the audience and its representation of their lives. The plays' relation to Church and society is discussed by Harris (1992).

19 In Chester the 'Water-leaders and Drawers in Dee' were in charge of *Noah's Flood*, in York it was the 'Fishers and Mariners'. 'The Fletchers, Bowyers, Coopers and Stringers' took hand of *Passion* in Chester, the 'Ironmongers' were responsible for *Crucifixion*, while in York it was the 'Pinners and Painters' who nailed Christ to the cross (Mills 1983).

20 More than two hundred plays are preserved. Cycles of plays are preserved from the towns of York (forty-eight plays) Chester (twenty-five plays), a town which probably is Wakefield (thirty-two plays) and from the unknown N-town (forty-one plays), which is the oldest of the cycles.

21 The Corpus Christi plays were called with English translations of *ludus*, the Latin word for 'play'. It shows that they were conceived of as 'play' and 'game', which means that they are not something done in earnest, and that drama was not seen as something distinctly different from other forms of human playing (Kolve 1966: 12–27).

22 The shepherds are usually cast as comic in the other Shepherds' plays as well (Kolve 1966: 145–74).

23 The quotes are taken from *Everyman and Medieval Miracle Plays*, Cawley (1990).

24 The connection between the symbolism of the Lord's Supper and the birth of Jesus had already been drawn by the Church Fathers. Bethlehem was interpreted as the 'bread-house', and visions of the child who was slaughtered by the angel, and its body cut up in small bloody morsels, were not uncommon.

25 The so-called Wakefield Master has been identified as the author of five other of the plays in the Wakefield cycle, where his talents as a comic author are abundantly shown.

26 The systematic doubling of things sacred and profane which the playwright so effectively carried through with his nativity play has no direct

parallel in the other shepherds' and nativity plays. That does not mean that *The Second Shepherds' Play* is the only comic play. Other shepherds' plays and nativity plays include comic actions of festival character as well – especially in connection with the shepherds' voluptuous, gargantuan meal before they get the angel's message (Chester, *The First Shepherds' Play* from Wakefield) and with the rude boy Trowle who brawls with the shepherds, scorns their food, wrestles with them and eventually wins over them all (Chester). The plays from York and N-town are not comic in the same way. The voluptous meal of the shepherd is symbolically pertinent because it is a comic realization of a big Christmas meal, and the overthrow of the shepherds can be seen as a casting down of the mighty. (See especially Kolve 1966: 'The invention of comic action'). Another comic action in nearly all these plays is the shepherds' bizarre parodies of the angel's song.

27 In *The Nativity* from N-town the second midwife, Salome, does not believe that Mary really is a virgin. Just as Thomas laid his hand in the side of Jesus because he doubted his resurrection from the dead, Salome probes Mary's virginity with her hand. Immediately the hand turns lame because of her disbelief. When she worships the new-born child and touches his clothes, the hand is restored. All the cycles include a sequence on the doubts of Joseph. The picture of Joseph as an old cuckold was common in many dramatic versions. He believes that Mary has been unfaithful, and therefore completely misunderstands what has happened. In other words, he seeks a natural explanation of supernatural events and does not understand the spiritual intervention which has taken place. Particularly in the play *Joseph* from N-town, Joseph is made into a ridiculous old fool with his pathetic appeal to other deceived husbands, his fright for being called impotent and his indignation over Mary and her maid who blame the angel (N-town 11, 71–4).

28 In the York cycle there are eight plays that resemble each other. On this basis critical scholarship concludes that they are the work of one author. He has been named the York Realist and is often ranked with the Wakefield Master. However, he (if he existed) probably did not rewrite *Crucifixion*, even if he wrote the plays which precede it (Y 26, 28–33) and one of those which follows immediately after (Y 36). (Cf. Robinson 1972, Davidson 1984, Richardson and Johnston 1991: 61–78.)

29 An explanation of this weight as the burden of sin is given by Paul Willis (1984).

30 Another matter is that the staging of the crucifixion with the raising of the cross with an actor on it would have demanded great technical skills from those involved.

31 This point is especially elaborated by Kolve (Kolve 1966: 175–205). Kolve points out how a new set of game words, as 'jape', 'jest', 'bourde' and 'layke' are introduced 'to describe the actions by which Christ is captured, brought to trial, buffeted, scourged, and killed' (180).

32 At the Fourth Lateran Council (1215) the transubtantiation doctrine became the official dogma of the Church. It got its scholastic formulation in the second part of that century from Thomas Aquinas: the substance of the bread and the wine were totally changed into the flesh

and blood of Christ while their external characteristics as bread and wine remained. A distinction is made between 'the substance', which is the changeable nature, and 'the accidents', the accidental qualities as smell, taste and appearance, which are not changed in the transubstantiation.

33 For the concepts of a 'sensory' and an 'ideological pole' in the symbol, see Turner 1975: 156–7.

6 MODERNITY AND THE REMYTHOLOGIZATION OF LAUGHTER: CHURCHLY BOREDOM AND THERAPEUTIC LAUGHTER

1 It has been pointed out that when Bakhtin postulates an opposition between the hierarchy and solemnity of the Church on the one hand and the carnival and laughter of the people on the other, this is an opposition which can be read in parallel to how Nietzsche described the contrast between the Apollonian and the Dionysian in Greek religion. Both were interested in religious origins. And similar to how Nietzsche argued for an aesthetification of the Dionysian processions in the tragedies, Bakhtin argued for a literarization of carnival in the novel (Nietzsche 1941; see Børtnes 1993: 117–30).

2 Eco refutes the Bakhtinian theory of carnival as actual liberation (Eco 1984).

3 For a discussion of the concept, see van der Horst 1978.

4 The leaflet, 'An invitation to join our "House of Laughter"' Michigan.

5 *The Joyful Noiseletter* started to come out in 1986. I have based my comments solely on the numbers from December 1993–December 1994 (8, 10–9, 10).

6 The editors draw attention, in small print on the back page, that 'The opinion expressed in this interdenominational newsletter are not always those of the editors or of God'.

7 See for instance titles like: *101 Things to do during a Dull Sermon* (Sims and Pegoda 1987); and *101 Things to do with a Dull Church: The Complete Guide for Bored Again Christians* (Wroe and Reith 1990).

8 Donald B. Lindsey and John Heeren have a different interpretation of the meaning of children's presence in comic pages with religious references. They say that even if children are portrayed as simple. innocent and inquisitive, the underside of their spiritual life is also put in view:

> Although it is probably unintended, cartoonists' depiction of these childish miscues indirectly evokes the theological dogma of original sin. The message sent by the number of these comics at least subtly implies that the most seemingly innocent among us carry their portion of this hereditary stain.
>
> (Lindsey and Heeren 1992)

9 Examples of newspaper headlines are: 'Spread of hysteria fad worries Church', *The Times*, 18 June 1994; 'Faithful fall for power of the spirit', 'Congregation rolling in the aisle', *Sunday Telegraph*, 19 June 1994; 'Rolling

in the aisles at church of laughter', *Daily Mail*, 20 June 1994; 'How charisma can corrupt Christianity', *Daily Mail*, 23 August 1995.

7 RELIGION OF JOKES: FLIRTATION WITH THE EAST

1　The scholarly world has recently rediscovered the value of Oriental laughter (Siegel 1987). The point is made (explicit or implicit) that Western thought has overlooked much of the value of humour (Morreall 1989).

2　The combination of divinity and baldness seems to be a general stumbling block – remember how Lucian, 1,800 years earlier, mocked 'the divine man' Alexander of Abonoteichos for wearing a toupee.

3　Laughter's significance has been commented upon by Bhagwan himself, his adherents and critics, while scholars have focused on laughter in the title of books and papers on the subject of Bhagwan Sri Rajneesh (Mullan 1983, Wallis and Bruce 1986).

4　1 What are four signs that Jesus was a nice Jewish boy?

He lived at home until He was 30. He went into his father's business. He thought His mother was a virgin. His mother thought He was God.

2 Why did the Rajneeshee cross the road?

To buy the other side.

3 What do you call a politician who never lies, never exaggerates, always does what he thinks is right and never listens to pressure groups?

A failure.

BIBLIOGRAPHY

Adkin, N. (1985) 'The Fathers on laughter', *Orpheus*, 6, 1: 149–52.

Alston, J. P. and Platt, L. A. (1968) 'Religious humor: a longitudinal content analysis of cartoons', *Sociological Analysis*, 30, 4: 217–22.

Ambrose, *Concerning Virgins*, in *A Select Library of Nicene and Post-Nicene Fathers*, second series, vol. 10, Edinburgh: T. & T. Clark, 1989.

Anderson, G. (1994) *Sage, Saint and Sophist*, London and New York: Routledge.

The Apocalypse of Peter (CG, VII, 3) J. M. Robinson (ed.) *The Nag Hammadi: Library in English*, Leiden: Brill, 1988, 372–8.

The Apocryphon of John (CG, II, 1, III, 1, IV, 1 and BG, 8502, 2), in J. M. Robinson (ed.) *The Nag Hammadi Library in English*, Leiden: Brill, 1988, 104–23.

Apollodorus, *The Library*, trans. J. G. Frazer, *Loeb Classical Library*, 2 vols, London: Heinemann, 1970–6.

Apuleius, *The Golden Ass*, trans. P. G. Welsh, Oxford: Clarendon Press, 1994.

Aristophanes, *The Frogs*, trans. B. B. Rogers, *Loeb Classical Library*, London: Heinemann, 1989.

Aristotle, *Nichomachean Ethics*, trans. H. Rackham, *Loeb Classical Library*, London: Heinemann, 1994.

—— *Poetics*, trans. W. Hamilton Fyfe, *Loeb Classical Library*, London: Heinemann, 1965.

Arnobius, *Adversus Nationes*, *Corpus scriptorum ecclesiasticorum*, Vindobonae: C. Geroldi, 1875.

—— *Rhetoric*, trans. J. H. Freese, *Loeb Classical Library*, London: Heinemann, 1959.

Ashley, K. M. (1979) '"Wyt" and "Wisdom" in N-town cycle', *Philological Quarterly*, 58: 121–35.

Augustine, *De Civitate Dei*, trans. W. M. Green, *Loeb Classical Library*, 7 vols, London: Heinemann, 1957–60.

Aung, S. Z. (1929) *Compendium of Philosophy*, London: Oxford University Press.

Backman, E. L. (1952) *Religious Dances in the Christian Church and in Popular Medicine*, Westport, Conn.: Greenwood Press.

Bakhtin, M. (1968) *Rabelais and his World*, Cambridge, Mass.: MIT Press.

Bartelink, G. J. M. (1994) *Athanase d'Alexandrie, Vie d'Antoine, introduction, texte critique, traduction, notes et index* (Sources Chrétiennes, no. 400), Paris: Les Editions du Cerf.

Basil, *Letters*, trans. R. J. Deferrari, *Loeb Classical Library*, 4 vols, London: Heinemann, 1961–2.

Bateson, G. (1953) 'The position of humor in human communication', in *Cybernetics*, New York: Macy Foundation, 1–47.

Belfrage, S. (1981) *Flowers of Emptiness*, London: Women's Press.

Benkor, S. (1980) 'Pagan criticism of Christianity during the first two centuries AD', *Aufstieg und Niedergang der Römischen Welt*, 23, 2: 1055–118.

Bergmann, W. (1985) 'Das Frühe Mönchtum als Soziale Bewegung', *Kölner Zeitschrift für Soziologie und Sozialpsychologie*, 37: 30–59.

Bergson, H. (1980) *Laughter: an Essay on the Meaning of the Comic*, in W. Sypher (ed.) *Comedy*, Baltimore: Johns Hopkins University Press.

Betz, H. D. (1959) 'Lukian von Samosata und das Christentum' *Novum Testamentum*, 3: 226–37.

—— (ed.) (1986) *The Greek Magical Papyri in Translation*, Chicago and London: University of Chicago Press.

Bharti, Ma Satya (1981) *Death Comes Dancing*, London: Routledge & Kegan Paul.

Bieler, L. (1935–6) *Theios Aner: Das Bild des 'göttlichen Menschen' in Spätantike und Frühchristentum*, 2 vols, Vienna: Oskar Höfel.

Bing, J. D. (1984) 'Adapa and immortality', *Ugarit-Forschungen*, 16: 53–6.

Black, M. (1983) 'An Aramaic etymology for Jaldabaoth?' in A. H. B. Logan and A. J. M. Wedderburn (eds) *The New Testament and Gnosis: Essays in Honour of Robert McL. Wilson*, Edinburgh: T. & T. Clark, 69–72.

Borgeaud, P. (1988) *The Cult of Pan in Ancient Greece*, Chicago and London: University of Chicago Press.

—— (1995) 'The rustic', in J.-P. Vernant (ed.) *The Greeks*, Chicago: University of Chicago Press, 285–98.

Børtnes, J. (1993) 'Bakhtin, Rabelais og det karnevaleske', in *Polyfoni og karneval*, Oslo: Universitetsforlaget.

Branham, R. B. (1989) *Unruly Eloquency: Lucian and the Comedy of Traditions*, Cambridge, Mass.: Harvard University Press.

Bremmer, J. (1992) 'Symbols of marginality from early Pythagoreans to late antique monks', *Greece and Rome*, 39, 2: 204–14.

Brenner, A. (1990) 'On the semantic field of humour, laughter, and the comic in the Old Testament', in Y. T. Radday and A. Brenner (eds) *On Humour and the Comic in the Hebrew Bible*, Sheffield: Almond Press, 39–58

Bröker, G. (1979) 'Lachen als Religiöses Motiv in Gnostischen Texten', in Peter Nagel (ed.) *Studien zum Menschenbild in Gnosis und Manichäismus*, Halle, Wittenberg: Martin Luther Universitat, 111–25.

Brown, C. G. (1989) 'Ares, Aphrodite, and the laughter of the gods', *Phoenix*, 43, 4: 283–93.

Brown, D. (1989) *The Body and Society: Men, Women and Sexual Renunciation in Early Christianity*, London and Boston: Faber & Faber.

Brumfield, A. C. (1981) *The Attic Festivals of Demeter and their Relation to the Agricultural Year*, Salem, NH: Ayer Company.

Brunnsåker, S. (1976) *Aspekter på Grekisk Konst*, vol. 1, Lund: Student litteratur, 124–31.

Buddhacarita of Asvaghosa, trans. E. H. Johnson, Delhi: Montilal Banarsidass, 1972.

Burkert, W. (1960) 'Das Lied von Ares und Aphrodite', *Rheinisches Museum für Philologie*, 103: 130–44.

—— (1972) *Homo Necans: Interpretationen altgriechischer Opferriten und Mythen*, Berlin: Walter de Gruyter.

—— (1985) *Greek Religion*, Oxford: Basil Blackwell.

—— (1992) *The Orientalizing Revolution: Neo Eastern Influence on Greek Culture in the Early Archaic Age*, Cambridge, Mass.: Harvard University Press.

Bynum, C. W. (1986) '". . . And Woman His Humanity": female imagery in the religious writing of the Later Middle Ages', in C. W. Bynum, S. Harrell and P. Richman, *Gender and Religion: On the Complexity of Symbols*, Boston: Beacon Press.

—— (1995) *The Resurrection of the Body in Western Christianity 200-1336*, New York: Columbia University Press.

du Cange, C. F. (1954) *Glossarium mediae et infimae Latinitatis*, Graz-Austria: Akademische Verlagsanstalt.

Carpenter, T. H. and Farone, C. A. (eds) (1993) *Masks of Dionysus*, Ithaca and London: Cornell University Press.

Carter, L. F. (1990) *Charisma and Control in Rajneeshpuram*, New York: Cambridge University Press.

Cawley, A. C. (ed.) (1990) *Everyman and Medieval Miracle Plays*, London: J. M. Dent & Son.

Chambers, E. K. (1954) *The Mediaeval Stage*, vol. 1, London: Oxford University Press.

Chapman, A. J. and Foot, H. C. (eds) (1977) *It's a Funny Thing – Humor*, Oxford: Pergamon Press.

Cicero, *De Natura Deorum*, trans. H. Rackham, *Loeb Classical Library*, London: Heinemann, 1967.

—— *De Officiis*, trans. W. Miller, *Loeb Classical Library*, London: Heinemann, 1961.

—— *De Oratore*, trans. E. W. Sutton, *Loeb Classical Library*, London: Heinemann, 1959.

—— *Orator*, trans. H. M. Hubbell, *Loeb Classical Library*, London: Heinemann, 1962.

Cixous, H. (1976) 'The laugh of the Medusa', *Signs: Journal for Women in Culture and Society*, 1, 41: 875–93.

Clement of Alexandria, *The Exhortation to the Greeks*, trans. G. W. Butterworth, *Loeb Classical Library*, London: Heinemann, 1982.

—— *Paidagogos: Christ the Educator*, trans. S. P. Wood, in *The Fathers of the Church*, vol. 23, Washington: Catholic University of America Press, 1954.

—— *Stromateis*, trans. John Ferguson, in *The Fathers of the Church*, vol. 85, Washington: Catholic University of America Press, 1991.

Corless, R. (1993) 'After Eliade, what?', *Religion*, 23, 4: 373–7.

Cormier, H. (1977) *The Humour of Jesus*, New York: Alba House.

Corrigan, K. (1986) 'Body and soul in ancient religious experience', in A. H. Armstrong (ed.) *Classical Mediterranean Spirituality*, London: Routledge & Kegan Paul, 360–83.

Cox, H. (1965) *The Secular City*, London: SCM Press.

—— (1969) *The Feast of Fools: A Theological Essay on Festivity and Fantasy*, New York and London: Harper & Row.

Curtius, E. R. (1953) *European Literature and the Latin Middle Ages*, London: Routledge & Kegan Paul.

Dahl, K. (1976) *Thesmophoria: En græsk kvindefest*, Copenhagen: Museum Tusculanum.

Dalley, S. (1989) *Myths from Mesopotamia*, Oxford and New York: Oxford University Press.

Dart, J. (1975) *The Laughing Saviour: The Discovery and Significance of the Nag Hammadi Gnostic Library*, New York: Harper & Row.

Davidson, C. (1984) 'The realism of the York realist and the York Passion', in P. Happé (ed.) *Medieval English Drama*, London: Macmillan, 101–17.

Detienne, M. (1977) *The Gardens of Adonis: Spices in Greek Mythology*, Hassocks, Sussex: Harvester Press.

—— (1979) *Dionysos Slain*, Baltimore: Johns Hopkins University Press.

—— (1989) 'The violence of wellborn ladies: women in the Thesmophoria', in M. Detienne and J.-P. Vernant (eds) *The Cuisine of Sacrifice among the Greeks*, Chicago and London: University of Chicago Press, 129–47.

Dhammapada, trans. S. Radhakrishnan, Madras: Oxford University Press, 1950.

Dillon, M. (1991) 'Tragic laughter', *Classical World*, 84: 345–55.

Douglas, M. (1970) *Natural Symbols: Explorations in Cosmobiology*, New York: Pantheon Books.

—— (1971) 'Do dogs laugh? A cross-cultural approach to body symbolism', *Journal of Psychosomatic Research*, 15: 387–90.

—— (1975) 'Jokes', in *Implicit Meanings: Essays in Anthropology*, London: Routledge & Kegan Paul, 94–114.

Dover, K. J. (1972) *Aristophanic Comedy*, Berkeley and Los Angeles: University of California Press.

Dreves, G. M. (1961) *Analecta Hymnica Medii Aevi*, 20, New York, 217–29.

—— (1983) *The Name of the Rose*, London: Secker & Warburg.

Eco, U. (1984) 'The frames of comic "freedom"', in U. Eco, V. V. Ivanov and M. Rector (eds) *Carnival!*, Berlin, New York and Amsterdam: Mouton, 1–9.

Elias, N. (1978) *The Civilizing Process*, vol. 1, *The History of Manners*, Oxford: Basil Blackwell.

Euripides, *Bacchae*, trans. R. Seaford, Warminster: Aris & Phillips, 1996.

Fehr, B. (1990) 'Entertainers at the Symposion: the Akletoi in the Archaic Period', in O. Murray (ed.) *Sympotica: A Symposium on the Symposion*, Oxford: Clarendon Press, 185–95.

Filoramo, G. (1992) *A History of Gnosticism*, Cambridge, Mass. and Oxford: Basil Blackwell.

Fingesten, P. (1970) 'The smile of the Buddha', in *The Eclipse of Symbolism*, Columbia: University of South Carolina Press, 52–66.

Finnestad, R. B. (1987) 'Egyptian thought about life as a problem of translation', in G. Englund (ed.) *The Religion of the Ancient Egyptians: Cognitive Structures and Popular Expressions*, BOREAS 20, Uppsala, 29–40.

Foley, H.P. (1985) *Ritual Irony: Poetry and Sacrifice in Euripides*, Ithaca and London: Cornell University Press.

—— (ed.) (1994) *The Homeric Hymn to Demeter: Translation, Commentary, and Interpretive Essays*, Princeton: Princeton University Press.

Forster, E. M. (1949) *A Passage to India*, London: Edward Arnold.

Foster, B. R. (1974) 'Humor and cuneiform literature', *Journal of the Ancient Near Eastern Society*, 6: 69–85.

Foucault, M. (1977) *Discipline and Punish: The Birth of the Prison*, London: Allen Lane.

—— (1990) *The Care of the Self*, vol. 3 of *The History of Sexuality*, Harmondsworth: Penguin.

Fox, R. L. (1988) *Pagans and Christians*, Harmondsworth: Penguin.

Frank, P. S. (1964) *Angelikos Bios*, Münster, Westfalen: Aschendorffsche Verlagsbuchhandlung.

Frazer, J. (1929) *The Golden Bough: A Study in Magic and Religion*, 2 vols, New York: Book League of America.

Freud, S. (1983) *Jokes and their Relation to the Unconscious*, Harmondsworth: Penguin.

Friedländer, P. (1934) 'Lachende Götter', *Die Antike*, 10: 209–26.

Fry, W. F. (1963) *Sweet Madness: A Study of Humor*, California: Pacific Books.

Fuchs, P. (1986) 'Die Weltflucht der Mönche: Anmerkungen zur Funktion des monastisch-aszetischen Schweigens', *Zeitschrift für Soziologie*, 15, 6: 393–405.

Garbini, G. (1988) *History and Ideology in Ancient Israel*, London: SCM Press.

Giddens, A. (1991) *Modernity and Self-Identity: Self and Society in the Late Modern Age*, Cambridge: Polity Press.

Gilhus, I. S. (1984) 'The Gnostic demiurge – an agnostic trickster', *Religion*, 14: 301–11.

—— (1985) *The Nature of the Archons: A Study, in the Soteriology of a Gnostic Treatise from Nag Hammadi (CG, II, 4)*, Wiesbaden: Otto Harrassowitz.

—— (1990) 'Carnival in religion, The Feast of Fools in France', *Numen*, 37, 1: 24–52.

—— (1991a) 'Laughter and blindness: a comparative study of structure and meaning in two Gnostic myths', in R. Skarsten, E. J. Kleppe and R. B. Finnestad (eds) *Understanding and History in Arts and Sciences: Studies in Honour of Richard H. Pierce*, Acta Humaniora Universitas Bergensis 1, Oslo: Solum Forlag, 59–67.

—— (1991b) 'Religion, laughter and the ludicrous', *Religion*, 21: 257–77.

Girard, R. (1977) *Violence and the Sacred*, Baltimore: Johns Hopkins University Press.

Grant, M. A. (1924) *The Ancient Rhetorical Theories of the Laughable: The Greek Rhetoricians and Cicero*, Madison, Wis.: University of Wisconsin.

Greene, H. C. (1931) 'The Song of the Ass', *Speculum: A Journal of Mediaeval Studies*, 6: 534–49.

Gugliemi, W. (1979) 'Humor in Wort und Bild auf altägyptischen Grabdarstellungen', in H. Brunner, R. Kannicht and K. Schwager (eds) *Wort und Bild*, Munich: Wilhelm Fink Verlag, 181–200.

—— (1980) 'Lachen', *Lexikon der Ägyptologie*, vol. 3, Wiesbaden: Otto Harrassowitz, 907–8.

Halliwell, S. (1991) 'The uses of laughter in Greek culture', *The Classical Quarterly*, 41, 2: 279–96.

Harris, J. W. (1992) *Medieval Theatre in Context*, London and New York: Routledge.

Hart, W. M. (1943) 'High comedy in the Odyssey', *University of California Publications in Classical Philology*, 12: 263–78.

Helterman, J. (1981) *Symbolic Action in the Plays of the Wakefield Master*, Athens, Georgia: University of Georgia Press.

Hennecke, I. E. and Schneemelcher, W. (1959) *Neutestamentliche Apokryphen*, Tübingen: J. C. B. Mohr.

Henrichs, A. (1982) 'Changing Dionysiac identities', in B. F. Meyer and E. P. Sanders (eds) *Jewish and Christian Self-Definition*, vol. 3, Philadelphia: Fortress Press, 137–60.

—— (1993) '"He has a god in him": human and divine in the modern perception of Dionysus', in T. H. Carpenter and C. A. Farone (eds) *Mask of Dionysus*, Ithaca and London: Cornell University Press.

Herodotus, *Historiae*, trans. A. D. Godley, *Loeb Classical Library*, 4 vols, London: Heinemann, 1957–66.

Hesiod, *Theogony*, trans. M. L. West, Oxford: Clarendon Press, 1966.

—— *Works and Days*, trans. M. L. West, Oxford: Clarendon Press, 1978.

Heyob, S. K. (1975) *The Cult of Isis among Women in the Graeco-Roman World*, Leiden: Brill.

Himmer, P. (1980) 'Oksen og æselet i og omkring fødselsfremstillinger', *Iconographisk Post*, 24–31.

Hobbes, T. (1973) *Leviathan*, London: Dent.

Hoffner, H. A., Jr (1990) *Hittite Myths*, Atlanta: Scholars Press.

Homer, *Iliad*, trans. A. T. Murray, *Loeb Classical Library*, 2 vols, London: Heinemann, 1961–3.

—— *Odyssey*, trans. A. T. Murray, *Loeb Classical Library*, 2 vols, London: Heinemann, 1984–5.

Hooff, J. van (1971) *Aspecten van het sociale gedrag en de communicatie bij humane an hogere niethumane primaten* (Aspects of the social behaviour and communication in human and higher non-human primates), Rotterdam: Bronder-Offset.

Horst, P. W. van der (1978) 'Is wittiness unchristian? A note on *eutrapelia* in Eph. v. 4', in T. Baarda, A. F. J. Klijn and W. C. van Unnik (eds) *Miscellanea Neotestamentica (Supplements to Novum Testamentum*, 48), Leiden: Brill, 163–77.

—— (1987) *Chaeremon: Egyptian Priest and Stoic Philosopher*, Leiden: Brill.

Hotchkiss, M. (1965) 'Sunday masks and pagan faces', *Religious Theatre*, 2: 59–76.

Huizinga, J. (1955) *The Waning of the Middle Ages*, London: Penguin.

—— (1970) *Homo Ludens: A Study of the Play Element in Culture*, London: Paladin.

Hvidberg, F. F. (1962) *Weeping and Laughter in the Old Testament: A Study of Canaanite–Israelite Religion*, Leiden and Copenhagen: Brill.

Hyers, C. (1974) *Zen and the Comic Spirit*, London: Rider Company.

—— (1981) *The Comic Vision and the Christian Faith: A Celebration of Life and Laughter*, New York: Pilgrim.

—— (1987) *And God Created Laughter: The Bible as Divine Comedy*, Atlanta: John Knox Press.

—— (1989) 'Humor in Zen: comic midwifery', *Philosophy East and West*, 39: 32.

The Hypostasis of the Archons (CG, II, 4), in J. M. Robinson (ed) *The Nag Hammadi Library in English*, Leiden: Brill, 161–9.

Irenaeus, *Against the Heresies*, book 1, trans. D. J. Unger in W. J. Burghardt, T. C. Lawler and John J. Dillon (eds) *Ancient Christian Writers*, New York: Paulist Press, 1992.

Jerome, *Selected Works: Letters*, in *A Select Library of the Nicene and Post-Nicene Fathers*, second series, vol. 6, Edinburgh: T. & T. Clark, 1989.

John Chrysostom, *Homilies on Galatians, Ephesians, Phillipians, Colossians, Thessalonians, Timothy, Titus, and Philemo*, in *A Select Library of the Nicene and Post-Nicene Fathers*, first series, vol. 13, Edinburgh: T. & T. Clark, 1994.

—— *Homilies on the Gospel of St. John, and Hebrews*, in *A Select Library of Nicene and Post-Nicene Fathers*, first series, vol. 14, Edinburgh, T. & T. Clark, 1989.

—— *On the Priesthood; Ascetic Treatises; Homilies and Letters; Homilies on the Statues*, in *A Select Library of the Nicene and Post-Nicene Fathers*, first series, vol. 9, Edinburgh: T. & T. Clark,1989.

Jonas, H. (1963) *The Gnostic Religion: The Message of the Alien God and the Beginnings of Christianity*, Boston: Beacon Press.

Jonsson, J. (1965) *Humour and Irony in the New Testament: Illustrated by Parallels in Talmud and Midrash*, Reykjavik: Bokautgafa Menningarsjods,1965.

Juvenal, *The Satires*, trans. G. G. Ramsay, *Loeb Classical Library*, London: Heinemann, 1965.

Kákosy, L. (1982) 'Mehet-weret', in *Lexikon der Agyptologie*, 4: 3–4.

Kapelrud, A. (1987) *The Violent Goddess: Anat in Ras Shamra Texts*, Oslo: Universitetsforlaget.

Kasantzakis, N. (1961) *Zorba, the Greek*, London: Faber and Faber.

Keel, O. and Uehlinger, C. (1993) *Göttinnen Götter und Gottessymbole: Neue Erkenntnisse zur Religionsgeschichte Kanaans und Israels aufgrund bislang unerschlossener ikonographischer Quellen*, Freiburg, Basel and Wien: Herder.

Khosroyev, A. (1995) *Die Bibliothek von Nag Hammadi: Einige Probleme des Christentums in Agypten während der ersten Jahrhunderte*, Altenberge: Oros Verlag.

Kienast, B. (1973) 'Die Weisheit des Adapa von Eridu', in M. A. Beek and A. A. Kampman *et al.* (eds) *Symbolae Bibliae et Mesopotamicae*, Leiden: Brill, 234–9.

King, K. (1990) 'Ridicule and rape, rule and rebellion: the Hypostasis of the Archons', in J. Goehrin, C. W. Hedrick, J. Sanders and H. D. Betz (eds) *Gnosticism and the Early Christian World*, Sonoma, Calif: Polebridge Press, 3–24.

Kirk, G. S. (1970) *Myth: Its Meaning and Functions in Ancient and Other Cultures*, Cambridge: Cambridge University Press.

Klijn, A. F. J. (1977) *Seth in Jewish, Christian and Gnostic Literature*, Leiden: Brill.

Koestler, A. (1964) *The Act of Creation*, London: Hutchinson and Co.

Kolve, V. A. (1966) *The Play Called Corpus Christi*, Stanford: Stanford University Press.

Kramer, S. N. and Maier, J. (1989) *Myths of Enki, the Crafty God*, New York and Oxford: Oxford University Press.

Kraus, F. R. (1960) 'Altmesopotamisches Lebensgefühl', *Journal of Near Eastern Studies*, 19: 117–32.

Kristeva, J. (1980) *Desire in Language: A Semiotic Approach to Literature and Art*, New York: Columbia University Press.

Kuschel, K.-J. (1994) *Laughter: A Theological Essay*, London: SCM Press.

Ladurie, E. Le Roy (1980) *Carnival: A People's Uprising at Romans*, 1579–1580, London: Scholar Press.

Lang, D. B. (1962) 'On the Biblical comic', *Judaism*, 11: 249–54.

Layton, B. (1986) 'The riddle of the Thunder (NHC V1, 2): the function of paradox in a Gnostic text from Nag Hammadi', in *Nag Hammadi, Gnosticism, and Early Christianity*, Peabody, Mass.: Hendrickson, 37–54.

—— (1987) *The Gnostic Scriptures*, New York: Doubleday & Co.

Legman, G. (1978) *No Laughing Matter: Rationale of the Dirty Joke*, second series, London and New York: Granada.

Leick, G. (1991) *A Dictionary of Ancient Near Eastern Mythology*, London: Routledge.

Lesko, L. H. (1991) 'Ancient Egyptian cosmogonies and cosmology', in B. E. Shafer (ed.) *Religion in Ancient Egypt*, London: Routledge, 87–122.

Lesky, A. (1961) 'Griechen lachen über ihre Götter', *Wiener humanistische Blätter*, 4: 30–40.

Lévi-Strauss, C. (1970) *The Raw and the Cooked*, vol. 1 of *Introduction to Mythology*, New York: Harper and Row.

de Liagre Böhl, F. M. Th. (1959) 'Die Mythe vom weisen Adapa', *Die Welt des Orients*, 2: 416–31.

Lichtheim, M. (1976) *Ancient Egyptian Literature*, vol. 2, Los Angeles and London: University of California Press.

Liddell, H. G. and Scott, R. (1968) *A Greek–English Lexicon*, Oxford: Clarendon Press.

Lindsey D. B. and Heeren, J. (1992) 'Where the sacred meets the profane: religion in the comic pages', *Review of Religious Research*, 34, 1: 63–77.

Lissarrague, F. (1990) 'The sexual life of satyrs', in D. M. Halperin, J. J. Winkler and F. I. Zeitlin (eds) *Before Sexuality: The Construction of Erotic Experience in the Ancient Greek World*, Princeton: Princeton University Press, 53–81.

Littre, E. (1958) *Dictionnaire de la langue française*, Paris: Editions universitaires.

Lorenz, K. (1963) *Das sogenannte Böse: Zur Naturgeschichte der Aggression*, Wien: Dr. G. Borotha-Scholer Verlag.

Loretz, O. (1990) *Ugarit und die Bibel: Kanaanäische Götter und Religion im alten Testament*, Darmstad: Wissenschaftliche Buchgesellschaft.

Lucian, *Complete Works*, trans. A. M. Harmon, K. Kilburn and M. D. MacLeod, *Loeb Classical Library*, 8 vols, London: Heinemann, 1913–67.

MacLeod, M. D. (1991) *Lucian: A Selection*, Warminster: Aris and Phillips.

MacMullen, R. (1981) *Paganism in the Roman Empire*, New Haven and London: Yale University Press.

Marcovich, M. (1988) 'Demeter, Baubo, Iacchus – and a redactor', in *Studies in Graeco-Roman Religions and Gnosticism*, Leiden: Brill, 20–7.

Meltzer, G. S. (1990) 'The role of comic perspectives in shaping Homer's tragic vision', *Classical World*, 83, 4: 265–80.

Merleau-Ponty, M. (1992) *Phenomenology of Perception*, London: Routledge.

Migne, J.-P. (1855) *Patrologiae cursus completus (Series Latina)*, vol. 207, Paris.

Milanezi, S. (1992) 'Outres enflées de rire: á propos de la fête du dieu Risus dans les "Métamorphoses" d'Apulée', *Revue de l'Histoire des Religions*, 229, 2: 125–47.

Miller, A. (1984) 'Ame no miso-ori-me (the heavenly weaving maiden): The Cosmic Weaver in early Shinto Myth and Ritual', *History of Religions*, 24, 1: 27–48.

Miller, P. C. (1993) 'The blazing body: ascetic desire in Jerome's letter to Eustochium', *Journal of Early Christian Studies*, 1, 1: 21–45.

—— (1994) 'Desert asceticism and "The body from nowhere"', *Journal of Early Christian Studies*, 2, 2: 137–53.

Mills, D. (1983) 'Appendix: manuscripts and contents of the extant English cycles', in A. C. Cawley, M. Jones, P. F. McDonald and D. Mills (eds) *The Revels History of Drama in English*, vol. 1, *Medieval Drama*, London and New York: Methuen, 292–301.

Milner, G. B. (1972) '*Homo ridens:* towards a semiotic theory of humour and laughter', *Semiotica*, 5: 1–30.

Minucius Felix, *Octavius*, trans. G. H. Rendall, *Loeb Classical Library*, London: Heinemann, 1984.

Moor, J. C. D. (1987) *An Anthology of Religious Texts from Ugarit*, Leiden: Brill.

Moore, A. (1977) *Iconography of Religions*, London: SCM Press.

Morreall, J. (1989) 'The rejection of humor in Western thought', *Philosophy East and West*, 39, 3: 243–65.

Mullan, B. (1983) *Life as Laughter: Following Bhagawan Shree Rajneesh*, London: Routledge & Kegan Paul.

Mullen, E. T., Jr (1986) *The Divine Council in Canaanite and Early Hebrew Literature*, Harvard Semitic Monographs 24, Chico, Calif.: Scholars Press.

Müller, H. P. (1983) 'Mythos als Gattung archaischen Erzählens und die Geschichte von Adapa', *Archiv für Orientforschung*, 29: 75–89.

Nash, W. (1985) *The Language of Humour: Style and Technique in Discourse*, London and New York: Longman.

Nietzsche, F. (1941) *Die Geburt der Tragödie aus dem Geiste der Musik*, Leipzig: Insel Verlag.

Nixon, L. (1995) 'The cults of Demeter and Kore', in R. Hawley and B. Levick (eds) *Women in Antiquity: New Assessments*, London: Routledge, 75–96.

Norden, E. (1924) *Die Geburt des Kindes*, Leipzig and Berlin: B. G. Teubner.

Olender, M. (1990) 'Aspects of Baubo', in D. M. Halperin, J. J. Winkler and F. I. Zeitlin (eds) *Before Sexuality: The Construction of Erotic Experience in the Ancient World*, Princeton: Princeton University Press, 83–113.

Oliver, J. P. (1980) 'The actuality of Lucian's Assembly of the Gods', *American Journal of Philology*, 101: 304–13.

Olson, C. (1990) *The Mysterious Play of Kali: An Interpretive Study of Ramakrishna*, Atlanta, Georgia: Scholars Press.

Origen, *Commentaire sur l'Evangile selon Matthieu*, Paris: Cerf, 1970.

—— *Contra Celsum*, trans. with an introduction and notes by H. Chadwick, London and New York: Cambridge University Press, 1980.

Otto, R. (1917) *Das Heilige: über das Irrationale in der Idee des Göttlichen und sein Verhältnis zum Rationale*, Breslau: Trewendt & Granier.

Ovid, *The Art of Love and other Poems*, trans. J. H. Mozley, rev. by G. P. Gold, *Loeb Classical Library*, London: Heinemann, 1962.

—— *Metamorphoses*, trans. F. J. Miller, *Loeb Classical Library*, 2 vols, London: Heinemann, 1958–60.

Patrides, C. A. (1983) 'The Biblical comic', *University of Toronto Quarterly*, 53, 1: 72–84.

Paulos, J. A. (1985) *I Think, Therefore I Laugh: An Alternative Approach to Philosophy*, New York: Columbia University Press.

Perkins, P. (1980) *The Gnostic Dialogue: The Early Church and the Crisis of Gnosticism*, New York: Paulist Press.

Petrus Cantor, *Verbum abbreviatum*, in J. P. Migne (ed.) *Patrologiae cursus completus (Series Latina)*, vol. 205, Paris, 1841–64.

Plato, *Laws*, trans. R. G. Bury, *Loeb Classical Library*, 2 vols, London: Heinemann, 1961.

—— *Philebus*, trans. H. N. Fowler, *Loeb Classical Library*, London: Heinemann, 1962.

—— *Republic*, trans. Paul Shorey, *Loeb Classical Library*, 2 vols, London: Heinemann, 1968–9.

Plutarch, *Lycurgus*, trans. B. Perrin, *Loeb Classical Library*, London: Heinemann, 1967.

—— *Romulus*, trans. B. Perrin, *Loeb Classical Library*, London: Heinemann, 1967.

Postman, N. (1993) *Amusing Ourselves to Death*, London: Methuen.

Prosser, E. (1961) *Drama and Religion in the English Mystery Plays: A Re-evaluation*, Stanford: Stanford University Press.

Quintilian, *Institutio Oratoria*, trans. H. E. Butler, *Loeb Classical Library*, 4 vols, London: Heinemann, 1959–63.

von Rad, G. (1972) *Genesis*, London: SCM Press.

Radday, Y. T. and Brenner, A. (eds) (1990) *On Humour and the Comic in the Hebrew Bible*, Sheffield: Almond Press.

Rahner, H. (1965) *Man at Play or Did You Ever Practice Eutrapelia?*, London: Burns & Oates.

Rajneesh, B. S. (1975) *Just Like That: Talks on Sufi Stories*, Bombay: Rajneesh Foundation.

—— (1980) *The Supreme Doctrine: Discourses on the Kenopanishad*, London: Routledge & Kegan Paul.

—— (1983) *The Orange Book: The Meditation Techniques of Bhagwan Shree Rajneesh*, Oregon: Rajneesh Foundation International.

—— (1989) *I Teach Religiousness, Not Religion*, Poona, India: Rebel Publishing House.

Raskin, V. (1985) *Semantic Mechanisms of Humor*, Dodrecht and Boston: D. Reidel.

Reines, C. W. (1972) 'Laughter in Biblical and Rabbinic literature', *Judaism*, 21: 176–83.

Resnick, I. M. (1987) '"Risus monasticus": laughter and Medieval monastic culture', *Revue Bénédictine*, 97, 1–2: 90–100.

Richardson C. and Johnston, J. (1991) *Medieval Drama*, London: Macmillan.

Robinson, J. M. (ed.) (1988) *The Nag Hammadi Library in English*, Leiden: Brill.

Robinson, J. W. (1972) 'The art of the York realist', in J. Taylor and A. H.

Nelson (eds) *Medieval English Drama: Essays Critical and Contextual*, Chicago and London: University of Chicago Press, 230–44.

Römer, W. H. Ph. (1978) 'Der Spassmacher im Alten Zweistromland', *Persica*, 7: 43–68.

Rosenthal, F. (1956) *Humor in Early Islam*, Philadelphia: University of Pennsylvania Press.

Roux, G. (1961) 'Adapa, le vent et l'eau', *Revue d'Assyrologie*: 13–33.

Rubin, M. (1991) *Corpus Christi: The Eucharist in Late Medieval Culture*, Cambridge: Cambridge University Press.

Rudhardt, J. (1992) 'Rires et sourires divins: essai sur la sensibilité religieuse des grecs et des premiers chrétiens', *Revue de théologie et de philosophie*, 124: 389–40.

Rudolph, K. (1978) *Die Gnosis: Wesen und Geschichte eines spätantike Religion*, Göttingen: Vandenhoeck & Ruprecht.

The Rule of the Master, trans. L. Eberle and C. Philippi, Kalamazoo, Mich.: Cistercian Publications, 1977.

The Rule of St. Benedict: In Latin and English with Notes, Colegeville, Minn.: Liturgical Press, 1981.

Salisbury, J. E. (1992) *Church Fathers, Independent Virgins*, London and New York: Verso.

Samra, C. (1986) *The Joyful Christ: The Healing Power of Humor*, New York: HarperCollins.

Sauneron, S. and Voyotte, J. (1959) 'La Naissance du monde selon l'Egypte ancienne', in *Sources Orientales*, Paris: Seuil, 2–91.

Sauren, H. (1988) 'Dieu rit: une interprétation du mythe d'Adapa', in A. Theodorides, P. Naster and J. Ries (eds) *Humor travail et science en Orient*, Leuven: Editions Peeters, 15–30.

Scarborough, J. (1991) 'The pharmacology of sacred plants, herbs, and roots', in C. A. Faraone and D. Obbink (eds) *Magika Hiera: Ancient Greek Magic and Religion*, Oxford and New York: Oxford University Press, 138–74.

Scholem, G. (1974) 'Jaldabaoth reconsidered', in *Mélanges de l'Histoire des Religions offerts a Henri-Charles Puech*, Paris: Presses universitaires de France, 405–21.

Schwarz, G. (1971) *Was Jesus wirklich sagte*, Vienna, Munich and Zürich: Verlag Fritz Molden.

Seaford, R. (1984) *Euripides: Cyclops*, Oxford: Clarendon Press.

—— (1996) *Euripides, Bacchae*, Warminster: Aris & Phillips.

The Second Treatise of the Great Seth (CG, VII, 2), in J. M. Robinson (ed.) *The Nag Hammadi Library in English*, Leiden: Brill, 1988, 362–71.

Segal, E. (1987) *Roman Laughter: The Comedy of Plautus*, New York and Oxford: Oxford University Press.

Seneca, *Epistulae Morales*, trans. R. M. Gummere, *Loeb Classical Library*, 3 vols, London: Heinemann, 1962.

Shershow, S. C. (1986) *Laughing Matters: The Paradox of Comedy*, Amherst: University of Massachusetts Press.

Shunyo, M. P. (1991) *Diamond Days with Osho*, Poona, India: Rebel Publishing House.

Siegel, L.(1987) *Laughing Matters: Comic Tradition in India*, Chicago and London: University of Chicago Press.

Sims T. and Pegoda D. (1987) *101 Things to do During a Dull Sermon*, Eastbourne: Minstrel/Monarch Publications.

Sloterdijk, P. (1983) *Kritik der zynischen Vernunft*, Frankfurt am Main: Suhrkamp Verlag.

—— (1989) *Eurotaoismus: Zur Kritik der politischen Kinetik*, Frankfurt am Main: Suhrkamp Verlag.

Smelik, K. A. D. and Hemelrijk, E. A. (1984) '"Who knows not what monsters demented Egypt worships?" Opinions on Egyptian animal worship in antiquity as part of the ancient conception of Egypt', *Aufstieg und Niedergang der Römischen Welt*, Berlin and New York: Walter de Gruyter, 17, 4: 1852–2000.

Smith, M. (1984) 'The eighth Book of Moses and how it grew', *Atti del XVII Congresso internazionale di papirologia*, Naples, 683–93

Smith, M. S. (1994) *The Ugaritic Baal Cycle*, vol. 1, Leiden: Brill.

Songe Möller, V. (1990) 'Pandoramyten: En ulykke kommer sjelden alene', *Nytt om kvinneforskning*, 3: 6–12.

Sørensen, J. P. (1991) 'Verdens ældste blasfemisag', *Chaos*, 16: 3–9.

Spencer, H. (1911) '*The physiology of laughter*', in *Essays on Education*, London: Dent.

Staines, D. (1991) 'The English Mystery Cycles', in S. Eckehard (ed.) *The Theatre of Medieval Europe*, Cambridge: Cambridge University Press, 80–96.

Stetkevych, S. P. (1996) 'Sarah and the hyena: laughter, menstruation, and the Genesis of a double entendre', *History of Religions*, 26, 3: 13–41.

Stroumsa, G. G. (1990) '*Caro salutis cardo*: shaping the person in early Christian thought', *History of Religions*, 30, 1: 25–50.

Suetonius, *The Lives of the Caesars*, trans. J. C. Rolfe, *Loeb Classical Library*, 2 vols, London: Heinemann, 1959.

Sulpicius Severus, *Vita Sancti Martini*, trans. J. Fontaine in *Sources Chretiennes*, Paris: Cerf, 1967–9, 133–5.

Süss, W. (1969) *Lachen, Komik und Witz in der Antike*, Zurich and Stuttgart: Artemis Verlag.

Swain, B. (1932) *Fools and Folly during the Middle Ages and the Renaissance*, New York: Columbia University Press.

Tertullian, *Apology* and *De Spectaculis* trans. T. R. Glover, *Loeb Classical Library*, London: Heinemann, 1984.

Thomas Aquinas, *Summa Theologica*, 3 vols, trans. Fathers of the English Dominican Province, New York: Benzinger Brothers.

Thomas, K. (1977) 'The place of laughter in Tudor and Stuart England', *Times Literary Supplement*, 21 January.

Thompson, J. and Heelas, P. (1986) *The Way of the Heart: The Rajneesh Movement*, Wellingborough, Northants: Aquarian Press.

Trueblood, E. (1964) *The Humor of Christ*, New York: Harper & Row.

Turner, J. D. (1986) 'Sethian Gnosticism: a literary history', in C. W. Hedrick and R. Hodgson, Jr (eds) *Nag Hammadi. Gnosticism and Early Christianity*, Peabody, Mass.: Hendrickson, 111–25.

Turner, P. (1990) *Lucian: Satirical Sketches*, Bloomington: Indiana University Press.

Turner, V. W. (1975) 'Symbolic studies', *Annual Review of Anthropology*, 4: 147–61.

Vermes, G. (1990) *The Dead Sea Scrolls in English*, Harmondsworth: Penguin.

Vernant, J.-P. (1990a) 'The myth of Prometheus in Hesiod', in *Myth and Society in Ancient Greece*, New York: Zone Books, 183–201.

—— (1990b) 'The masked Dionysus of Euripides' Bacchai', in J.-P. Vernant and P. Vidal-Naquet (eds) *Myth and Tragedy in Ancient Greece*, New York: Zone Books, 381–412.

—— (1991) 'Greek religion, ancient religion', in F. I. Zeitlin (ed.) *Mortals and Immortals: Collected Essays*, Princeton: Princeton University Press, 269–89.

—— (1995) *The Greeks*, Chicago and London: University of Chicago Press.

Versnel, H. S. (1990) 'Eis Dionysos: the tragic paradox of Bacchae', in *Ter unus: Isis, Dionysos, Hermes: Three Studies in Henotheism*, Leiden: Brill, 96–205.

—— (1993) *Transition and Reversal in Myth and Ritual*, Leiden: Brill, 235–60.

Villetard, H. (1911) 'Remarques sur la Fête des Fous au Moyen Age', Paris: A. Picars et fils, 1–28.

Virgil, *Eclogues*, trans. H. R. Fairclough, *Loeb Classical Library*, London: Heinemann, 1967.

Vos, N. (1966) *The Drama of Comedy: Victim and Victor*, Richmond: John Knox.

de Vries, G. J. (1985) 'Laughter in Plato's writings', *Mnemosyne*, 38, 3–4: 378–81.

van de Walle, B. (1969) *L'Humour dans la littérature et dans l'art de l'ancienne Egypte*, Leiden: Nederlands instituut voor het nabije oosten.

Wallis, R. and Bruce S. (1986) 'Religion as fun? The Rajneesh movement', in *Sociological Theory, Religion and Collective Action*, Belfast: Queen's University Press, 191–224.

Walter, N. (1990) *Blasphemy: Ancient and Modern*, London: Rationalist Press Association.

Ward, B. (trans.) (1981) *The Sayings of the Desert Fathers (Apophthegmata Patrum)*, Oxford: Mowbrays.

Welsh, P. G. (1994) *Apuleius: The Golden Ass*, Oxford: Clarendon Press.

West, M. L. (1966) *Hesiod, Theogony*, Oxford: Clarendon Press.

—— (1974) *Studies in Greek Elegy and Iambus*, Berlin: Walter de Gruyter.

—— (1978) *Hesiod: Works and Days*, Oxford: Clarendon Press.

Wilken, R. L. (1984) *The Christians as the Romans Saw Them*, New Haven and London: Yale University Press.

Willis, P. (1984) 'The weight of sin in the York *Crucifixio*', *Leeds Studies in English*, 15: 109–16.

Winkler, J. J. (1990) *The Constraints of Desire: The Anthropology of Sex and Gender in Ancient Greece*, New York and London: Routledge.

—— and Zeitlin F. (eds) (1990) *Nothing to Do with Dionysos? Athenian Drama in Its Social Context*, Princeton: Princeton University Press.

Wisse, F. (1980) 'Stalking those elusive Sethians', in B. Layton (ed.) *The Rediscovery of Gnosticism*, Leiden: Brill, 563–76.

Wood, F. T. (1940) 'The comic element in the English Mystery Plays', *Neophilologus*, 25: 194–206.

Woolf, R. (1972) *The English Mystery Plays*, Berkeley and Los Angeles: University of California Press.

—— (1984) 'The Wakefield shepherds' plays', in P. Happé (ed.) *Medieval English Drama*, London: Macmillan, 89–95.

Wroe, M. and Reith, A. (1990) *101 Things to do with a Dull Church: The Complete Guide for Bored Again Christians*, Eastbourne: Minstrel/Monarch Publications.

Zaidman, L. B. and Pantel, P. S. (1992) *Religion in the Ancient Greek City*, Cambridge: Cambridge University Press.

Zeitlin, F. I. (1982) 'Cultic models of the female: rites of Dionysus and Demeter', *Arethusa*, 15: 129–57.

INDEX